THE PICTURE OF DORIAN GRAY

Oscar Wilde

AUTHORED by Jon Carter
UPDATED AND REVISED by Jordan Berkow

COVER DESIGN by Table XI Partners LLC
COVER PHOTO by Olivia Verma and © 2005 GradeSaver, LLC

BOOK DESIGN by Table XI Partners LLC

Published by GradeSaver LLC, www.gradesaver.com

First published in the United States of America by GradeSaver LLC. 2005

GRADESAVER, the GradeSaver logo and the phrase "Getting you the grade since 1999" are registered trademarks of GradeSaver, LLC

ISBN 978-1-60259-077-9

Printed in the United States of America

For other products and additional information please visit
http://www.gradesaver.com

Table of Contents

Table of Contents

Biography of Oscar Wilde (1854–1900)

Oscar Wilde was born in 1854 in Dublin, Ireland, to prominent intellectuals William Wilde and Lady Jane Francesca Wilde. Though they were not aristocrats, the Wildes were well–off, and provided Oscar with a fine education. Oscar was especially influenced by his mother, a brilliantly witty raconteur, and as a child he was frequently invited to socialize with her intellectual circle of friends.

Wilde entered Trinity College in 1871 and focused his academic studies on the classics and theories of aestheticism. In 1874, he transferred to Oxford and studied under the divergent tutorials of John Ruskin (a social theorist and Renaissance man) and Walter Pater (a proponent of the new school of aestheticism). Wilde negotiated their conflicting philosophies as his personal life developed. He also experimented with cutting–edge fashion and experimented with homosexuality.

Upon graduating from Oxford, Wilde had a brief flirtation with Catholicism, but his independent orientation toward the world prevented an exclusive attachment to religion. In 1881, he published his first volume of verse (*Poems*), and he became famous enough to be satirized in a Gilbert and Sullivan comic opera. He moved to Chelsea, an avant–garde neighborhood in London, but his father's death and the family's snowballing debts forced him to embark on a lecture tour of the United States in 1882. Upon arriving at customs, Wilde made his now–famous statement: "I have nothing to declare except my genius." On tour, he dressed in a characteristically flamboyant style. He advocated for the philosophy of the Aesthetic: art should exist solely for art's sake, or, as he wrote elsewhere, it should be "useless." While on tour in New York, Wilde also produced his first, unsuccessful play, *Vera*.

In 1884, Wilde married a shy and wealthy Irishwoman named Constance Lloyd, and the two moved into a posh house in London. Wilde briefly edited *Woman's World* magazine while writing a collection of fairy tales and a number of essays (collected later as *Intentions*, 1891,) which elaborated his unique approach to Aestheticism, a movement with which he was rather reluctant to associate himself. While Wilde had been socially and professionally linked to confirmed aesthetes such as Max Beerbohm, Arthur Symons, and Aubrey Beardsley, he was an open critic of the kind of reductive aesthetic philosophy expressed in the famous journal *The Yellow Book*. Preferring to explore his own thoughts about art and politics through idiosyncratic readings of Plato, Shakespeare, and contemporary painting, Wilde's social circle featured a diverse cast of characters, among them poets, painters, theater personalities, intellectuals, and London "rent boys" (male prostitutes). His closest friend, however, remained the Canadian critic and artist Robert Ross, who at times handled Wilde's publicity and acted as Wilde's confidant in his professional and personal affairs.

Throughout the 1890s, Wilde became a household name with the publication of his masterpiece novel, *The Picture of Dorian Gray*, a Faustian tale about beauty and youth, as well as a string of highly successful plays, including *Lady Windermere's Fan* (1892), the Symbolist melodrama *Salome* (1892), *A Woman of No Importance* (1893), and *An Ideal Husband* (1895). His last play, *The Importance of Being Earnest* (1895), among his greatest, is considered the original modern comedy of manners. By this time, Wilde's extravagant appearance, refined wit, and melodious speaking voice had made him one of London's most sought–after dinner party guests.

In 1891, Wilde became infatuated with the beautiful young poet Lord Alfred Douglas (known as "Bosie"). The dynamic between Bosie and Wilde was unstable at the best of times, and the pair often split for months before agreeing to reunite. Still, the relationship consumed Wilde's personal life, to the extent that the sexual nature of their friendship had become a matter of public knowledge. In 1895, Douglas's father, the Marquess of Queensbury, accused Wilde of sodomy. Wilde replied by charging Queensbury with libel. Queensbury located several of Wilde's letters to Bosie, as well as other incriminating evidence. In a second trial often referred to as "the trial of the century," the writer was found guilty of "indecent acts" and was sentenced to two years of hard labor in England's Reading Gaol.

In 1897, while in prison, Wilde wrote *De Profundis*, an examination of his newfound spirituality. After his release, he moved to France under an assumed name. He wrote *The Ballad of Reading Gaol* in 1898 and published two letters on the poor conditions of prison. One of the letters helped reform a law to keep children from imprisonment. His new life in France, however, was lonely, impoverished, and humiliating.

Wilde died in 1900 in a Paris hotel room. He retained his epigrammatic wit until his last breath. He is rumored to have said of the drab establishment that between the awful wallpaper and himself, "One of us has to go." Critical and popular attention to Wilde has recently experienced a resurgence; various directors have produced films based on his plays and life, and his writings remain a wellspring of witticisms and reflections on aestheticism, morality, and society.

About The Picture of Dorian Gray

The Picture of Dorian Gray, Oscar Wilde's first and only novel, is a faustian story of a man who trades the purity of his soul for undying youth. It was written in 1889 and first published in the literary magazine *Lippincott's Monthly* in July, 1890 (Drew ix). This was a shorter version, without the preface or chapters 3, 5, or 15–18, which were added for later publication in 1891. These additional chapters, which are now indespensible aspects of the work, introduce the character of James Vane, the vengeful brother of one of the victims of Dorian's many careless affairs. At the time it was published, the novel elicited a sensational amount of negative criticism, with detractors condemning its homosexual undertones and seeming embrace of hedonistic values. The preface was written as a response to the unkind critics of the first edition, blaming them for failing to grasp Wilde's belief that art should be appreciated on purely aesthetic terms, without consideration of morality.

The central idea behind Wilde's reinterpretation of the Faust myth appeared several years before he began writing the novel, in the form of a spoken tale that the author would tell to friends, especially young admirers. Wilde was well aware of the story's debt to older tales of selling one's soul, youth, beauty, and power, freely admitting that it was a notion "that is old in the history of literature, but to which I have given a new form" (Drew xiv). This "new form" brings the idea of duplicity, of leading a double life, to the forefront of the tale, a theme that is much more dominant in *Dorian Gray* than it is in Marlowe's *Doctor Faustus* or Goethe's *Faust*, which is a typical characteristic of Wilde's work. This theme is explicitly explored, for instance, in the author's most celebrated play, *The Importance of Being Earnest*.

As Wilde's notoriety grew, mainly as a result of this novel's infamy, his enemies continued to use the homosexual undertones and seemingly immoral hedonistic values of *Dorian Gray* as an argument against his character. Such criticisms continued throughout his ruinous court appearances in 1895. At the time, any sort of homosexual act was a serious criminal offense in England. The first published version of the book from *Lippincott's Monthly* contained much more obvious allusions to physical love between Dorian and Lord Henry, and Dorian and Basil. Wilde had made a point of reducing these references in the revision, but the original version of the novel provided much fuel for his opponents' arguments.

After the trials, Wilde was briefly imprisoned, and his literary career never recovered. He moved to the European mainland and lived under an assumed name until his death, in a Paris hotel, in 1900. Wilde cited this novel as being primarily responsible for his ruin, speaking of "the note of Doom that like a purple thread runs through the cold cloth of *Dorian Gray*" (Drew xxvii). Only decades after Wilde's death would the work truly become respected as a literary masterpiece.

Despite the critical preoccupation with the book's seeming approval of alternative lifestyles, *Dorian Gray* is a novel that offers much more to both intellectual and artistically sensitive readers. It is primarily concerned with examining the complex relationships between life, art, beauty, and sin, while presenting a compellingly cynical portriat of high society life in Victorian–era London. It examines the role of art in social and personal life while warning against – despite Wilde's claims of artistic amorality – the dangers of unchecked vanity and superficiality.

Character List

Basil Hallward

A reclusive painter much respected by the London aristocracy. He admires Dorian to the point of adulation and paints many portraits of him, finally creating his masterpiece, the titular picture. Basil introduces Dorian to Lord Henry Wotton.

Lord Henry Wotton

A champion of sensual pleasure, notorious among London's high society for his dazzling conversation and brazenly immoral views. He values beauty above all else, and is chiefly responsible for Dorian's corruption.

Dorian Gray

A physically beautiful young man, naive and good-hearted until corrupted by vanity. Dorian makes a faustian bargain: his body remains young and beautiful, while his portrait alters to reflect his age and increasingly guilty conscience. He eventually seems to bring corruption, pain, and death to all inhabitants of the social circles in which he moves.

Lord George Fermor

Henry Wotton's uncle, an idle, impatient aristocrat. Henry calls on him to elicit information about Dorian's background. He is a portrait of a typical self-centered, elderly aristocrat whose money allows him to devote his life to purely fanciful and superficial endeavors.

Sybil Vane

A beautiful, 17-year-old Shakespearean actress, and Dorian's first love. The pair are smitten with each other and are engaged to be married until Dorian sees her perform badly, and, disillusioned, treats her with extreme cruelty. Broken-hearted, she commits suicide.

Mrs Vane

Sybil's aging, single mother. Mrs Vane is also an actress, and both she and her daughter struggle to support their small family through their craft. She is most comfortable when her real life is as melodramatic as it is on the stage.

James Vane

Sibyl's younger, fiercely protective brother, who leaves England to become a sailor. He is suspicious of his sister's lover from the start, and swears to hunt the man down if he causes her any harm. After Sibyl's death, he dedicates himself to finding his sister's "Prince Charming", and is eventually killed by a wayward hunting bullet while trying to take his revenge on Dorian.

Mr Isaacs

The man who runs the decrepit theater where Sybil performs. The Vanes are deeply in debt to him. He is a sterotypical portrait of an old Jewish man, whom Dorian and Basil find contemptible, and whom Lord Henry finds amusing.

Victor

Dorian's faithful first servant, of whom he is unnecessarily suspicious. Victor has been replaced by another servant by the second half of the novel, although the details of his dismissal are never disclosed. We are left to surmise that either Dorian's paranoia became too great, or that Victor eventually grew unable to bear his master's increasingly corrupt nature.

Mr Hubbard

A celebrated London frame–maker whom Dorian calls upon to help him hide the portrait in the attic. He appears only once in the novel, but stokes Dorian's growing paranoia by being puzzled when the protagonist adamantly refuses to uncover the painting for him to see it.

Adrian Singleton

A promising young member of society whose life takes a turn for the worse when he befriends Dorian. Adrian ends up addicted to opium, spending all of his time and money in filthy, dilapidated drug dens.

Alan Campbell

A talented chemist and musician who is close to Dorian until their friendship comes to a bitter end as a consequence of Dorian's increasingly bad reputation. Dorian forces him to assist in the disposal of Basil's body using blackmail, and Alan later commits suicide.

Lady Narborough

The widow of a wealthy man, and the mother of richly married daughters. She hosts a great many parties, and is very fond of Dorian and Lord Henry.

Sir Geoffrey Clouston

A London socialite and guest of Lady Narborough who shoots James Vane in a hunting accident. Unlike most of the aristocrats present at the incident, he appears to be quite disturbed by the idea of having taken a human life.

Lady Alice Chapman

Lady Narborough's decidedly unremarkable daughter, a minor character whom Wilde uses to display Lord Henry's superficiality.

Duchess of Monmouth

Gladys, a clever and pretty young aristocrat who nearly matches Lord Henry in conversational wit. She freely and lightly admits to numerous adulterous affairs, and flirts with Dorian at one of his parties.

Hetty Merton

A beautiful young village girl who falls in love with Dorian and reminds him of Sybil Vane. Dorian consciously – and hypocritically – refrains from corrupting her in an attempt to begin living a good life, and to purify his soul. She does not believe Dorian when he tells her that he is wicked, because he looks so young and innocent. She is the last young woman with whom Dorian is romantically linked.

Major Themes

Art as a Mirror

This theme is exemplified by the titular portrait. Dorian Gray's image reflects his conscience and his true self, and serves as a mirror of his soul. This fact echoes Wilde's statement (found in the preface) that "It is the spectator...that art really mirrors." However, this theme first appears earlier in the preface, with Wilde's contention that "the nineteenth–century dislike of realism is the rage of Caliban seeing his own face in a glass." Realism is a genre of artistic expression that is said to have shown the 19th century its own reflection. The fear that Dorian expresses when viewing the painting, and the emotions that he seeks to escape through sin, drug addiction, and even murder, might be considered an expression of his rage at laying eyes upon his true self. The idea of reflectivity also recalls a major mythical influence on the novel: the story of Narcissus. Dorian, like Narcissus, falls in love with his own image, and is ultimately destroyed by it.

The Art of Living (or Living through Art)

This theme is expressed most prominently in the character of Lord Henry, and in the "new hedonism" he espouses. Lord Henry openly approaches life as an art form, seeking to sculpt Dorian's personality, and treating even his most casual speeches as dramatic performances. Most notably, he pursues new sensations and impressions of beauty with the amorality of an artist: as Wilde writes in the preface, "No artist has ethical sympathies." This latter characteristic is the one that leaves the deepest impression on Dorian's character. However, although both men fancy themselves artists at living, their flaw lies in their blatant violation of the rule given in the first line of the preface: "To reveal art and conceal the artist is art's aim." Dorian and Lord Henry both strive to reveal themselves in their "art."

Wilde also explores this theme by blurring the line between life and art. Characters in the novel include actresses who live as though they are constantly on stage, and a painter who values a friendship predominantly because the relationship improves his ability to paint. Dorian himself consciously bases his life and actions on a work of art: a book given to him by Lord Henry.

Vanity as Original Sin

Dorian's physical beauty is his most cherished attribute, and vanity is, as a consequence, his most crippling vice. Once a sense of the preciousness of his own beauty has been instilled in him by Lord Henry, all of Dorian's actions, from his wish for undying youth at the beginning of the novel to his desperate attempt to destroy the portrait at the end, are motivated by vanity. Even his attempts at altruism are driven by a desire to improve the appearance of his soul. Throughout the novel, vanity haunts Dorian, seeming to damn his actions before he even commits them; vanity is his original sin. Dorian's fall from grace, then, is the consequence of his decision to embrace vanity – and indeed, all new and pleasurable feelings – as a virtue, at the behest of Lord Henry, his corrupter. In the preface to the novel, Wilde invites us to ponder the inescapability of vanity in our own relationship to art when he states that "it is the spectator, and not life, that art really mirrors." If we see ourselves in art, and find art to be beautiful, then it follows that we, like Dorian, are in fact admiring our own beauty.

The Duplicity of One's Public and Private Selves

This theme is prominent in much of Wilde's work. It plays a central role in *The Importace of Being Earnest*, and is prominent throughout this novel, as well. In addition to the protagonist, many of the novel's characters are greatly concerned with their reputations. Lord Henry and Basil Hallward both counsel Dorian on how to best preserve his good status in the public eye. When crimes are committed, it is not personal absolution that anyone is concerned with, but whether or not the guilty party will be held responsible by the public. In this way, each character in the novel possesses an awareness of a split identity: one that is defined by the public, and one that they define themselves. The figure of Dorian is an allegorical representation of this condition. The portrait is a literal visualization of Dorian's private self, the state of his soul, while Dorian himself looks perpetually young, beautiful, and innocent.

Much of Wilde's social commentary in the novel springs from his manipulation of this theme. People's responses to Dorian constantly highlight the overwhelming superficiality of Victorian London (if not people in general). Because Dorian always looks innocent, most of the people he encounters assume that he is a good, kind person. Dorian literally gets away with murder because people are automatically more willing to believe their eyes than anything else.

The Value of Beauty and Youth

Lord Henry claims to value beauty and youth above all else. It is this belief, when imparted to Dorian, that drives the protagonist to make the wish that ultimately damns him. When Dorian realizes that he will keep his youthful appearance regardless of whatever immoral actions he indulges in, he considers himself free of the moral constraints faced by ordinary men. He values his physical appearance more than the state of his soul, which is openly displayed by the ever–increasing degradation of the portrait. This superficial faith in the ultimate value of youth and beauty is therefore the driving mechanism behind the protagonist's damnation. In this way, *The Picture of Dorian Gray* may be read as a moralistic tale warning against the dangers of valuing one's appearance too highly, and of neglecting one's conscience.

It is important to bear in mind that the beauty that Dorian incessantly pursues is a beauty defined by a purely artistic sensibility, as opposed to a humanitarian one. When faced with the news of his fiance's suicide, Dorian views the event as satisfyingly melodramatic. His obsession with aesthetic beauty prevents Dorian from attending to the pangs of his own conscience.

Influence and Corruption

Dorian begins the novel as an innocent youth. Under Lord Henry's influence he becomes corrupt, and eventually begins corrupting other youths himself. One of the major philosophical questions raised by this novel is that of where to locate the responsibility for a person's misdeeds. If one engages in a moralistic reading, *The Picture of Dorian Gray* can be seen as a lesson in taking responsibility for one's actions. Dorian often points to Lord Henry as the source of his corruption. However, when contemplating the plights of others, Dorian lays the blame at their own feet rather than considering the role that he might have played in their downfall.

Homosexuality

This is the theme that Wilde was alluding to when he wrote of the "note of Doom that like a purple thread runs through the cold cloth of *Dorian Gray*" in a letter to his young lover, Bosie, following his ruinous court appearances. He calls the theme of homosexuality a "note of doom" because sodomy and homosexuality in general were severly punishable offenses in Victorian England, and it was under such charges that Wilde was brought to trial.

In the novel, there are strong homosexual undertones in the relationships between the three central characters (Dorian, Lord Henry, and Basil Hallward), as well as between Dorian and several of the young men whose lives he is said to have "ruined", most notably Alan Campbell. In his revision of the novel for its official release, after it appeared in *Lippincott's Monthly Magazine*, Wilde removed all of the most blatant references to homosexuality. However, the idea of sexual affection between men proved too integral to the characters and their interactions to be entirely expunged from the novel. This theme has prompted many critics to read the novel as the story of a man's struggle with his socially unacceptable proclivities. Indeed, some feel that Wilde was working out his own conflicted feelings on the subject through the novel.

Glossary of Terms

Adonis

a figure from Greek mythology, a mortal said to represent the pinnacle of physical beauty and athletic perfection

ague

coldness, or shivering

antinomianism

heretical Christian belief holding that predestination frees people from morality

asphodel

a white flower that symbolizes death, as ancient mythology holds that it covers the Elysian fields

Bacchante

a priestess of Bacchus, the Roman god of wine ("Dionysus" in Greek), whose worship may take the form of drunken revelry or murderous blood lust

beater

a man responsible for driving game into a hunter's line of sight by beating plants and bushes with a stick

bismuth

a metal–based whitening powder used primarily as theatrical make–up

Blue–book (or "English Blue–book")

a book listing the names and addresses of important people, such as government officials; like a selective telephone directory

broughams

covered carriages used as cabs for the wealthy in Victorian London

Caliban

the uneducated, brutish savage enslaved by Prospero in Shakespeare's *The Tempest*

cassone

a small chest, or strongbox

chaudfroid

meat or fish served in gelatin; a French delicacy

cope

a broad, rounded cloak worn by priests and other members of the clergy during church processions

dandy

a word used amongst members of British high society in Wilde's day to describe a fashionable young man with effeminate affectations

doctrinaire

a derogatory term for an intellectual who is doggedly devoted to the theories and ideas of others

dowager

a rich widow

ennui

the French word for boredom

ensconced

settled securely; surrounded by

esprit

the French word for liveliness, spiritedness, or sprightliness

fop

see "dandy"

frangipanni

a strong, exotic perfume

gamekeeper

a man employed by an estate to care for the birds and other animals that are kept for hunting purposes

Ganymede

a figure from Greek mythology; a beautiful young boy chosen by Zeus to be the cup–bearer of the gods

Grosvenor

mentioned by Lord Henry in conversation with Basil, it refers to The Grosvenor Gallery, which in Wilde's day was a newer, more progressive venue for art than The Royal Academy

hautboy

oboe

hedonism

a doctrine from ancient Greece stating that the pursuit of pleasure is life's greatest aim; Lord Henry's form of "new hedonism," a popular term during Wilde's life, was a variation on this idea, holding that the pursuit of new sensations through art takes precedence above all else

high stocks

high, stiff collars worn by fashionable men

idolatrous

adoring something excessively, bordering on or exceeding worship

iniquities

transgressions or sins

jarvies

nineteenth century slang for coach drivers

languid

nonchalant, apathetic, and lacking energy; Wilde often uses this word to describe the mannerisms of his characters, especially Lord Henry

lithe

flexible; supple

Louis–Quinze

an ornate style of fashion and furniture named after Louis XV of France

moue

a pout or frown

nacre

pearl, or mother–of–pearl

narcissism

the love of one's own appearance; named for Narcissus, a figure from Greek mythology who fell in love with his reflection in a pond, was drowned when he tried to embrace it, and was transformed into a narcissus flower.

nocturne

a musical composition with a dark, reflective, dreamy atmosphere

obelisk

a tall, rectangular object that tapers to a point at the top

opium den

a place, generally located in a slum, where opium is bought and smoked, usually along with other illicit activities, such as prostitution and gambling. Opium use was common among artists of the romantic period, and retained its popularity well into Wilde's day

paradox

a true statement that seems to contradict itself

parseme

a French word meaning strewn or speckled

precis

a French word indicating a synopsis of important facts

protege

a French word referring to a person under the tutelage of a master or mentor; an apprentice

salon

a French word for "living room" that is used to denote a regular social gathering of artists and intellectuals

sudaria

a highly decorative, fringed ceremonial handkerchief

The Academy

mentioned by Lord Henry in the first chapter, The Academy refers to The Royal Academy of Arts, one of Britain's oldest societies of fine art. The Academy was known for its support of conservative taste at the time of the novel's publication

The Bristol

a fancy, expensive London hotel

victoria

a small, covered carriage

Short Summary

Dorian Gray meets Lord Henry Wotton at the studio of Basil Hallward, who is using Dorian as a model for his latest painting. Lord Henry tells Dorian about his epicurean views on life, and convinces him of the value of beauty above all other things. The young and impressionable Dorian is greatly moved by Lord Henry's words. When Basil shows them the newly completed painting, Dorian is flooded with awe at the sight of his own image, and is overwhelmed by his fear that his youth and beauty will fade. He becomes jealous that the picture will be beautiful forever while he is destined to wither and age. He passionately wishes that it could be the other way around. Lord Henry is fascinated with Dorian's innocence as much as Dorian is impressed by Henry's cynically sensual outlook on life. They become fast friends, to Basil's dismay. He fears that Henry will be a corrupting influence on the young, innocent Dorian, whom he adores.

Dorian and Lord Henry become fast friends, often dining together and attending the same social functions. Henry's influence has a profound effect on the young man, who soon adopts Henry's views as his own, abandoning ethical restraints and seeing life in terms of pleasure and sensuality. Dorian falls in love with the beautiful Sybil Vane, a poor but talented young Shakespearean actress. They are engaged to be married until Dorian brings Henry and Basil to a performance, where her acting is uncharacteristically – and inexplicably – terrible. Dorian confronts Sybil backstage, and she tells him that since she is now truly in love, she no longer believes in acting. Disgusted and offended, Dorian breaks off their engagement and leaves her sobbing on the floor. When he returns home, he discovers that the figure in his portrait now bears a slightly different, more contemptuous facial expression.

Dorian awakens late the next day feeling guilty for his treatment of Sybil, and writes an impassioned love letter begging her forgiveness. Soon, however, Lord Henry arrives, and informs Dorian that Sybil committed suicide last night. Dorian is shocked and wracked with guilt, but Henry convinces him to view the event artistically, saying that the superb melodrama of her death is a thing to be admired. Succumbing to the older man's suggestion, Dorian decides that he need not feel guilty, especially since his enchanted portrait will now bear his guilt for him. The picture will serve as his conscience, allowing him to live freely. When Basil visits Dorian to console him, he is appalled at his friend's apathy towards Sybil's death. Dorian is unapologetic and annoyed by Basil's adulation of him.

Paranoid that someone might discover the secret of the painting, and therefore the true nature of his soul, Dorian hides the image in his attic. Over the next several years, Dorian's face remains young and innocent, despite his many selfish affairs and scandals. He is an extremely popular socialite, admired for his fine taste and revered as a fashionable trend–setter. The picture, however, continues to age, and grows more unattractive with each foul deed. Dorian cannot keep himself from looking at the picture periodically, but he is appalled by it, and is only truly happy when he manages to forget its existence. He immerses himself in various obsessions, studying mysticism, jewelry, music, and ancient tapestries. These interests, however, are all merely distractions that allow him to forget the hideousness of his true soul.

One night, Basil visits Dorian to confront him about all of the terrible rumors he has heard. The painter wants to believe that his friend is stll a good person. Dorian decides to show him the portrait so that he can see the true degradation of his soul, but when Basil sees it he is horrified, and urges his friend to repent for his sins. Basil's reaction enrages Dorian, and he murders the artist with a knife. To dispose of the body, he blackmails an estranged acquaintance, Alan Campbell, a chemist who is able to burn the body in the attic's fireplace. Alan has already been driven into isolation by Dorian's corrupting influence, and this action eventually compels him to commit suicide.

Not long after, Dorian visits an opium den and is attacked by James Vane, Sybil's brother, who has sworn revenge on the man that drove his sister to suicide. 18 years have passed since the event, however, yet Dorian still looks like a 20–year–old youth. James thinks that he is mistaken, and Dorian escapes before his would–be murderer learns the truth. Over the next several days Dorian lives in fear, sure that James is searching for him. While hunting one day, Dorian's friend Geoffrey accidentally shoots a man hiding on Dorian's property. This stranger is revealed to be James Vane. Dorian is overcome with relief, but cannot escape the fact that four deaths now weigh on his conscience.

Deciding to change his life for the better, Dorian commits a good deed by refusing to corrupt a young girl who has fallen in love with him. He checks the portrait, hoping to find that it has changed for the better, but when he realizes that the only thing that has changed is the new, hypocritical smirk on the wrinkled face, he realizes that even his effort to save his soul was driven by vanity. In a fit of despair, he decides to destroy the picture with the same knife that he used to kill Basil, its creator. Downstairs, Dorian's servants hear a shriek, and rush upstairs to find their master dead on the floor, the knife plunged into his own chest. Dorian's youthful countenance is gone, and his servants are only able to recognize him by the jewelry on his fingers.

Summary and Analysis of the Preface &Chapters 1 &2

Summary

The preface is a collection of free–standing statements that form a manifesto about the purpose of art, the role of the artist, and the value of beauty. Signed by Oscar Wilde, the preface serves as a primer for how Wilde intends the novel to be read. He defines the artist as "the creator of beautiful things," and the critic as "he who can translate into another manner or new material his impression of beautiful things." He condemns anyone who finds ugliness where there is beauty as "corrupt." He states that a book can be neither moral or immoral, and that morality itself serves only as "part of the subject matter" of art. Since art exists solely to communicate beauty, Wilde warns against reading too much into any work of art: "Those who go beneath the surface do so at their peril." The preface ends with the whimsical statement that "All art is quite useless"; earlier, however, we are told that the "only excuse for making a useless thing is that one admires it intensely."

Chapter 1 opens with a description of Basil Hallward, a respected but reclusive painter, who is entertaining his friend, Lord Henry Wotton. It is a beautiful spring day. Lord Henry admires Basil's latest work–in–progress, a full–length portrait of a beautiful young man, and urges him to show it at a gallery. Basil says that he never will because he has "put too much of myself into it." Lord Henry laughs at him, mistaking his meaning, and says that the painter is nothing like the boy in the picture. In the following discussion, it becomes clear that Lord Henry often speaks in elaborate, cynical, even paradoxical aphorisms, while Basil is a simpler man with more purely romantic values. Basil clarifies his earlier statement by saying that "every portrait that is painted with feeling is a portrait of the artist, not of the sitter."

The discussion turns towards the sitter, whom Basil describes as a delightfully pure and naive young man named Dorian Gray. Lord Henry insists on meeting the man, but Basil refuses. He wants to protect the boy's innocent purity from Lord Henry's cynical, sensualist influence. It becomes clear that Basil has very strong feelings for Dorian, bordering on adulation. To Basil's chagrin, the butler announces Dorian's unexpected arrival, and the artist implores of Lord Henry: "He has a simple and a beautiful nature...Don't spoil him...Don't take away from me the one person who gives my art whatever charm it posseses."

Lord Henry and Dorian are introduced, and begin talking as Basil prepares his paints and brushes. Henry is immediately taken by the boy's charm and good looks, and Dorian is quickly impressed with Henry's conversational acumen and firmly unorthodox views of morality. Controlling his jealousy, Basil asks Henry to leave so that Dorian can pose for the picture in peace. Dorian insists that Henry stay, Basil relents, and Henry continues to dazzle the model with an impromtu lecture on how people ought to be less inhibited so that one might "realise one's nature perfectly."

As he paints, Basil notes that "a look had come into the lad's face that he had never seen before." It is this look of revelation that the artist captures in his painting. Lord Henry's lecture makes Dorian feel that "entirely fresh influences were at work within him," and he marvels that "mere words" could have this effect. Lord Henry sees clearly the effect that he has on Dorian, and is proud of it. Dorian and his new friend adjourn to the garden as Basil puts the finishing touches on his work. In the garden, Henry tells the boy that "Nothing can cure the soul but the senses, just as nothing can cure the senses but the soul," and that he has "the most marvellous youth, and youth is the one thing worth having." The conversation then turns towards beauty, and Henry asserts that it has "the divine right of soverignity," that beauty gives power to those who have it, and that nothing in the world is greater. He warns Dorian that his beauty will someday fade, a prospect that horrifies the impressionable young man.

Basil then informs the pair that the painting is complete. Upon seeing the painting, Dorian is overwhelmed with joy and wonder at its beauty. It is his first unabashed immersion into vanity. As soon as he thinks of how precious his beauty is, however, he remembers Lord Henry's statement about the fleetingness of youth and flies into a fit, becoming enraged at the portrait because it will always retain its beauty, while he is destined to grow old. In a fit of passion, he thinks, "If only it were the other way! If only it were I who was to be always young, and the picture was to grow old! For that...I would give my soul for that!" Seeing Dorian's distress, Basil grabs a knife and moves to destroy the painting. Dorian stops him, saying that it would be murder, and that he is in love with the work. Basil promises to give the picture to Dorian as a gift, and tells him that it will be delivered to him as soon as it is dried and lacquered.

Lord Henry is fascinated by Dorian's behavior, and the two make plans to go to the theater together that night. Basil objects, and asks Dorian to dine with him instead. Dorian declines and leaves with Lord Henry, saying that he will call on Basil tomorrow.

Analysis

The preface was not included in the first printings of the novel, but was added later by Wilde as a direct response to accusations of immorality and indecency. Several of the statements made in the preface are thus purely defensive: for example, Wilde writes that "When critics disagree the artist is in accordance with himself." However, the preface also establishes many of the novel's major themes and provides the reader with a means of interpreting different aspects of the story.

The opening chapters introduce us to the novel's major players. We learn a great deal about Lord Henry, Basil, and Dorian, and are provided with information that will inform the development of the story. The ways that Wilde portrays each character's personality are particularly notable. For instance, the reader meets the incomplete portrait of Dorian before Dorian himself even makes his first appearance. Dorian exists as a beautiful but essentially superficial image first and foremost, even before he exists as a human being. After all, the title of the book is *The Picture of Dorian*

Gray, suggesting that the novel is about the image of the man, rather than about the man himself. In this manner, Wilde begins to blur the distinction between man and image (a practice that begins in earnest when the picture comes to reflect the true nature of Dorian's soul), raising questions as to the true location of one's identity, and the value of superficiality. Lord Henry remarks that "It is only shallow people who do not judge by appearances" (21), and Wilde offers the reader no choice but to do so in this instance. Like Basil, who seems more smitten with Dorian as a model than as a person, like Lord Henry, who claims to value beauty above all else, and like Victorian society in general, the book itself seems more concerned with the image of the protagonist than with the man himself.

At times, both Basil and Lord Henry seem to ascribe to ideals consistent with those of the author. Basil asserts that "there is nothing that art cannot express"; is a direct rephrasing of the line "the artist can express everything" from the preface. Lord Henry's habit of constantly spouting "profound" aphorisms and his languid, sensual personality recall Wilde's own social persona. However, to assume that either character is intended to be read as a representation of Wilde himself is a fallacy. Both characters also express opinions that directly contradict with the beliefs found in the preface; a fact that becomes clearer as the novel progresses.

Basil's reclusiveness is mentioned early on almost as an afterthought, but plays an important role later in the novel. Since he customarily withdraws from society on a regular basis, his absence is unremarkable when he eventually disappears for good. Another notable aspect of Basil's character is his personal devotion to Dorian. There are a number of indications that the painter is smitten with Dorian on more than a professional level. These feelings, based on Dorian's beauty and purity, eventually lead to rejection by the boy, and ultimately to Basil's alleged inability to create any more great art.

The second chapter, in which Dorian himself makes his first appearance, describes the beginning of Dorian's corruption at the hands of Lord Henry. It also introduces Dorian's inadvertantly faustian bargain, as the boy pleads for the picture to age in his place. Worth noting is the fact that Lord Henry invites Dorian into Basil's garden as he delivers his lecture on youth, beauty, and the value of immorality. This Eden–like setting emphasizes the fact that Dorian's response to Henry's words represents the boy's fall from grace; it is Dorian's original sin.

Dorian's initial response to the portrait recalls the statement made in the preface that "Those who find ugly meanings in beautiful things are corrupt without being charming." The painting is a masterpiece, certainly a "beautiful thing," but the image sparks jealousy and hatred in Dorian because it reminds him of the fleeting nature of his own youth. He is already "corrupt without being charming," but this marks the starting point of his steady fall from grace. Basil's attempt to destroy the painting with a knife, and Dorian's exclamation that "It would be murder" foreshadows the events that take place in chapters 13 and 20.

Summary and Analysis of Chapter 3

Summary

The next day, at "half–past twelve", Lord Henry visits his uncle, the grumpy Lord George Fermor, to learn what he can about Dorian Gray's past. Lord Fermor is old and idle, having spent most of his life moving apathetically through London's aristocratic social circles, devoting himself "to the serious study of the great aristocratic art of doing absolutely nothing." He is therefore an ideal resource for information concerning people's private lives. All Lord Henry has to do is mention that Dorian "is the last Lord Kelso's grandson."

Lord Fermor informs his nephew that Dorian's mother was Margaret Devereux, the beautiful daughter of Lord Kelso, who upset her father and caused a scandal by eloping with a poor man of a lower class. Lord Kelso, a bitter man, sought his revenge by paying a young Belgian to insult his unwanted son–in–law. Dorian's father was apparently killed in the resulting fight, and his mother died only several months later. The specific conditions of the deaths are never disclosed. Custody of Dorian fell to Lord Kelso, who was socially ostracized for causing the whole ordeal. Kelso was notoriously mean–spirited and quarrelsome, always making scenes by viciously haggling with cabmen and the like.

Henry leaves Lord Fermor's home to attend a luncheon at the house of his aunt, Lady Agatha. On the way, he reflects on how fascinating he finds the story of Dorian's origin, thinking that it makes his life "a strange, almost modern, romance." Henry is excited by the prospect of shaping the young man's personality by opening his eyes to the world of sensuality that Henry is so devoted to. He thinks that the boy "could be fashioned into a marvelous type," and that "He would dominate him…He would make that wonderful spirit his own." At this point, we learn just how manipulative Henry truly is.

Henry arrives at the lunch gathering rather late, as is his custom. Once at the table, he soon dominates the conversation, impressing the guests with the cleverness of his speech and playfully offending them with the beliefs that "To get back one's youth, one has merely to repeat one's follies," and that people "discover when it is too late that the only things one never regrets are one's mistakes." The man's charming tirade is described in terms of juggling and acrobatics. Dorian is among the guests, and Henry is performing primarily for his sake.

His efforts are not in vain: once the lunch is finished, Dorian approaches him with words of admiration, saying that "No one talks so wonderfully as you do." He accompanies Lord Henry to the park instead of calling on Basil as he had promised.

Analysis

Instead of being driven by friendly affection, Henry is interested in Dorian as an artistic or scientific project. Dorian's purity and innocence are, to him, a blank canvas on which he can paint a personality so as to lead Dorian towards a lifestyle that Henry finds artistically pleasing. This is a prominent thread in the novel's thematic exploration of the relationship between life and art. That Henry refers to Dorian's early life as "a strange, almost modern, romance" is indicative of the man's need to view life in artistic, as opposed to ethical, terms. (The coldness of this need will be even more damning to Henry's character later, in his interpretation of Sybil Vane's suicide.)

Henry fancies himself an artist, a sculptor or painter of personalities; he uses his charm, wit, and scandalous views as his paintbrush or chisel. Nevertheless, as curious as he is to see Dorian's character evolve into its own fascinating shape, Henry's deepest motivation is unabashedly selfish and vain. He wants to "be to Dorian Gray what, without knowing it, the lad was to the painter." He wants to be adored, and to turn Dorian into a more physically attractive version of himself. This echoes the belief expressed in the preface that "the only excuse for making a useless [i.e. "artistic"] thing is that one admires it intensely." However, although he certainly admires it, Henry's "art" is fundamentally flawed according to the first line of the preface: "To reveal art and conceal the artist is art's aim." Henry wants his "art" (Dorian) to reveal the "artist" (himself). This suggests another major theme that explores the value of superficiality and the discrepancy between one's interior self and how one is perceived by others.

As far plot development, this chapter offers very little. We learn crucial information about Dorian's past, facts that inform our assessment of his character, making him seem more tragic and romantic than he might otherwise. However, most of its pages are devoted to a colorful description of the people and the conversation at Lady Agatha's lunch table. Indeed, Henry's conversational acrobatics in this chapter are the closest example we have of Wilde's own conversational style.

However, this is not to suggest that the content of this chapter is extraneous. All of Henry's witticisms also reverberate strongly with the major themes of the novel. For instance, Henry remarks that he "can sympathise with everything, except suffering...One should sympathise with the colour, the beauty, the joy of life. The less said about life's sores the better." This sentiment, of course, exemplifies Dorian's later outlook on life, when his "sores" are concealed within the portrait.

Henry also states that "I can stand brute force, but brute reason is quite unbearable. There is something unfair about its use. It is hitting below the intellect." Witty word play aside, this is a pithy expression of a central tenet of the Victorian Age's "New Hedonism." Feelings, sensations, and emotions were considered important, not cold intellectualism. Once again, Henry voices a notion that will dominate Dorian's actions later in the novel.

Summary and Analysis of Chapter 4

Summary

A month later, Dorian pays a visit to Henry, finding his wife at home. She is pleased to meet the man with whom her husband has become so preoccupied. After Dorian's comment that one is obligated to engage in conversation when bad music is being performed, she remarks that "that is one of Harry's views…I always hear Harry's views from his friends, that is the only way I get to know them." Henry (or "Harry") arrives, and his wife exits. Henry tells Dorian never to marry a woman as sentimental as his wife, a trait which he blames on the fairness of her hair.

Dorian delivers the news that he has come to share: he is in love with a girl named Sybil Vane. She is an actress who plays all of the young leading female roles at a theater devoted solely to Shakespeare's works. The theater and the rest of the cast are of very poor quality, but Sybil is apparently a brilliant actress and stunningly beautiful. Dorian went backstage to meet her after the third performance he had attended, and found her to be completely unaware of her own skill, seemingly unable to separate real life from that of the stage. He tells Henry that she prefers to call him "Prince Charming," because, as Dorian says, "She regarded me merely as a person in a play. She knows nothing of life." This purity and naiveté is indescribably charming to Dorian: he has fallen madly in love, and tells Henry that he worships Sybil and that she is the only thing that matters to him.

Dorian convinces Henry to come with him to see her play Juliet in the next day's production. Henry says that he will invite Basil. At the mention of the painter's name, Dorian remarks that he feels guilty for having ignored the painter for several weeks, since he appreciates the masterful portrait despite being "a little jealous of the picture for being a whole month younger than I am."

The conversation turns towards the character of artists, and Henry insists that the better the artist, the duller his personality, and that only truly terrible artists are worth spending time with. Dorian eventually takes his leave. Later that night, Henry returns home to find a telegram from Dorian informing him that he and Sybil are engaged to be married.

Analysis

This chapter describes a key moment in the development of Dorian's personality. Henry is not jealous of Dorian's fascination with another person, but pays careful attention to Dorian's impression of his own emotional state. Recognizing his influence at work on the boy brings "a gleam of pleasure into his brown agate eyes"; he is like an artist proudly admiring his work. Henry's views are elucidated by the statement that "a complex personality…was indeed, in its way, a real work of art." Henry's beliefs are delivered in the voice of the narrator; this technique, called "free indirect discourse", is one that Wilde frequently used.

The nature of Dorian's love reflects Henry's devotion to life as art. Sybil is described as almost completely devoid of her own personality, and only able to behave as if she is in a play. Dorian is in love with the characters she plays, with her talent, and with her beauty, but not with her. He values everything superficial about her, as is revealed when she tries to show her true self to him.

Early in their conversation, after telling Henry how much he treasures his words and trusts his judgment, Dorian states, "If ever I did a crime I would confess it to you. You would understand me." This boldly foreshadows later events in the novel, and is also an indication of the commencement of Dorian's degradation. The young man that was innocent and good–hearted only a month before now freely considers criminal actions for the sake of having a new sensation, without giving a single thought to the possibility of a guilty conscience.

Dorian criticizes Sybil for treating him like a person in a play, but is blind to the fact that he has fallen in love with the characters she plays, and hardly even knows the girl herself. Dorian has begun to whole–heartedly devote himself to artistic ideals, mistakenly assuming that they are his reality. Indeed, when Sybil begins to show a glimmer of the person behind her characters, Dorian's reaction is not very pleasant. Earlier, however, he doesn't even hesitate to propose to a girl he hardly knows; a testament to his misguided devotion to artistry and artifice.

Henry realizes the error of Dorian's ways, but instead of pointing them out for the sake of his friend's well–being, he anticipates the fun he will have observing the repercussions. Dorian's blossoming self–centeredness is a successful manifestation of Henry's influence. Interestingly, this is the first chapter in which Dorian actually has more dialogue than Henry. Until this point, we have witnessed Dorian's reactions only through Henry's eyes, and through narrative comments. Dorian only actually begins to take the spotlight once his corruption is underway.

Summary and Analysis of Chapter 5

Summary

Sybil Vane tells her mother all about her love for Dorian, but only refers to him as "Prince Charming," since she has promised not to disclose his true name to anyone. Mrs Vane is greatly distressed over her daughter's well–being and the family's financial status. She reminds Sybil that they owe money to Mr Isaacs, the theater owner, but Sybil doesn't care about anything but her Prince Charming. Mrs Vane is full of affectations, always seeming to behave as if she is on stage.

Sybil's younger brother James enters, wanting to walk with his sister and bid farewell to his mother, as he is leaving for Australia to become a sailor. James is not an actor, and hates the city and the stage. He is a very serious, stocky young man. It is his hope that he will never have to return to London, and will make enough money to keep his mother and sister from having to act. When Sybil leaves to prepare for their walk, James urges his mother to protect her. He is very jealous, protective of his sister, and suspicious of the situation, since Sybil doesn't even seem to know her suitor's name. Mrs Vane reminds her son that Prince Charming is a gentleman, and that it could be a very profitable marriage for the family.

Sybil returns, and the siblings leave. On their walk, other people stare at them because Sybil's beauty contrasts with James's stocky, disheveled appearance. Sybil romanticizes her brother's life as a sailor: she is sure that he will find gold in a distant land, fight off robbers, and rescue a beautiful heiress. James is distressed about his sister's affair, and tells her that he doesn't trust her suitor.

Sybil defends Dorian, always referring to him as "Prince Charming", and tells James that he will only understand her feelings once he falls in love himself. Sybil spots Dorian riding by and James runs to see what he looks like, but the carriage drives off. James states, "I wish I had [seen him], for as sure as there is a God in heaven, if he ever does you any wrong, I shall kill him." Sybil scolds her brother for being bad–tempered, and doesn't take his threat seriously.

After returning home for dinner, James tells his mother that "if this man ever wrongs my sister, I will find out who he is, track him down, and kill him like a dog." The melodrama of the statement and the theatrical manner of its delivery make Mrs Vane admire her son, because she is only truly comfortable when life mimics the theater. James's departure, however, disappoints her, because the potentially heart–jerking farewell "was lost in vulgar details" of haggling with a cab driver.

Analysis

This is one of the few chapters in the novel that does not focus primarily on Dorian or Lord Henry. Like the preface, and all of the later chapters dealing with James

Vane, this chapter was absent from the original version of the novel printed in *Lippincott's Monthly*. This fact is made apparent from the tone of writing: by introducing three new characters that barely interact with the main players of the story, this chapter seems to deviate from the plot.

However, Wilde does use the Vanes to further explore the complex relationship between life and art. Sybil and her mother both seem to be stuck in theatrical mentalities. This is most striking in the character of Mrs Vane, who is actually disappointed when the events in her life don't live up to the melodrama of the theater. She appreciates Sybil's love–stricken outbursts because they are worthy of the stage. When James enters their room, "she mentally elevated her son to the dignity of an audience. She felt sure that the tableau was interesting." She is disappointed with the farewell of her only son, because "It was crude. It reminded her of a bad rehearsal." To Mrs Vane, life has become a shadow of her art.

Sybil is similarly afflicted, but to a lesser degree. The theatricality of her actions can be attributed to her naiveté and the intensity of her love for Dorian. This love exists in the real world, and thus saves Sybil from the need to feel that she is constantly in a play. Ironically, this desire to live in the "real world" and experience true love eventually leads to her death.

The threats made by James, which are dismissed by Sybil as byproducts of the over–zealousness of youth, return to haunt Dorian in the later chapters (specifically chapters 15–18). James comes to represent the inescapable consequences of Dorian's past transgressions. The threats that Sybil finds so harmless and endearing prove to be earnest declarations of intent.

When Dorian drives by in a carriage, unseen by James but noticed by Sybil, Wilde is emphasizing the discrepency between their social classes. Dorian rides in an expensive carriage, while the Vanes walk the filthy streets. This discrepency is the source of much of James's rage and frustration, and also Sybil's tragically idealistic hopes for a better life.

Summary and Analysis of Chapters 6 &7

Summary

Lord Henry and Basil Hallward discuss Dorian's engagement at the painter's house. They are planning to dine with Dorian before going to see Sybil's performance that night. Basil can't believe that Dorian is really engaged, saying that Dorian "is far too sensible" to make such a rash decision. To this, Henry replies that "Dorian is far too wise not to do foolish things now and then." Basil is taken aback by Henry's detached, artistic fascination with Dorian's life. The artist disapproves of Dorian's actions, and is worried about the boy's emotional health; Henry, however, is delighted, knowing that whatever the outcome is, it will be greatly entertaining.

Dorian arrives, insisting that he be congratulated. Basil says that was hurt to hear about the engagement from Henry, and not from Dorian himself. Henry quickly changes the subject. Dorian wants Basil to approve of his actions, saying "I have been right, Basil, haven't I, to take my love out of poetry, and to find my wife in Shakespeare's plays?" Basil reluctantly agrees with Dorian. When Henry cynically remarks about the business–like nature of marriage, Basil objects, saying that Dorian "is not like other men. He would never bring misery upon anyone. His nature is too fine for that." Henry continues to philosophize about the nature of women and how they act when in love. To him, "Women treat us just as humanity treats its gods. They worship us and are always bothering us to do something for them." Dorian is sure that Sybil's acting will put an end to Henry's cynicism and reconcile all disagreements between the three men. When they see her perform, they will be too overwhelmed by her beauty to consider anything else. The three men leave to see the play, *Romeo and Juliet*.

The theater is surprisingly crowded that night. Once seated in their box, Lord Henry observes the obnoxious, unrefined behavior of the lower–class theatergoers. Basil comforts Dorian against Henry's cynicism. The play begins, and they all note that the orchestra is terrible. Finally, Sybil appears on stage. She looks beautiful, but acts terribly. Her voice is exquisite, but "from the point of view of tone" is "absolutely false." Dorian is horrified and confused. The other two men are disappointed, but are too polite to make any remarks. Her performance, usually the one saving grace in the theater's otherwise dreadful productions, only gets worse as the play progresses. After the second act, the audience hisses, and Dorian's guests stand to leave. Basil tries to comfort the boy, saying that Sybil must be ill, and that he shouldn't be upset, since "Love is a more wonderful thing than art" anyway, to which Henry replies that "They are both simply forms of imitation". Dorian is inconsolable. Henry tells him to cheer up, since "the secret of remaining young is never to have an emotion that is unbecoming."

The two men leave, and Dorian forces himself to suffer through the rest of the performance. Afterwards, he rushes backstage to confront Sybil. She is delighted to see him and surprised at his anger, since she had assumed that he would know the reason for her terrible performance. When he demands to be told why she performed badly, she tells him that having met him, she can no longer believe in the theater. Before Dorian, she says, "acting was the one reality of my life," and now he has "freed my soul from prison" and "taught me what reality really is." Having experienced true love, she says, "it would be profanation for me to play at being in love." Dorian is horrified, disgusted, and completely unable to love her anymore. She can't believe it, and when he pulls away from her touch, she falls to the floor, groveling at his feet. Dorian feels repulsion rather than empathy, and leaves her sobbing on the floor.

Strangely numb and unable to come to terms with Sybil's lost talent or his unexpected callousness towards her, Dorian aimlessly wanders the city until dawn. He returns home, where he happens to glance at Basil's portrait, and is puzzled to find that the facial expression is slightly different: there seems to be "a touch of cruelty in the mouth." He rubs his eyes and changes the lighting, but is certain that the picture has changed. The cruelty in the expression reminds him of his cruelty to Sybil, but he feels wronged for the misery that she has caused him with her bad acting, and consoles himself by thinking that "women were better suited to bear sorrow than men…When they took lovers, it was merely to have someone with whom they could have scenes. Lord Henry told him that, and Lord Henry knew what women were." Unable to make any sense of the picture's transformation, he realizes, after much pondering, that "It held the secret of his life, and told his story…changed or unchanged, [it] would be to him the visible emblem of conscience." Exhausted, he covers the portrait with a screen, and goes to sleep.

Analysis

Dorian's relationship with Sybil is the first major casualty of the devotion to sensual pleasure inspired by Lord Henry. Valuing artistic beauty above all else allows Dorian to confuse his love for Sybil's acting with a love for Sybil herself. She seems to be the perfect wife, because Dorian believes that she can offer him all of Shakespeare's heroines in a single body. Indeed, Dorian remarks to Basil that he has "had the arms of Rosalind around me, and kissed Juliet on the mouth." Dorian's love is a means of escaping reality; therefore, Sybil's awareness of "what reality really is" is unacceptable.

His resulting cruelty towards her is the first undeniable mark of the corruption of Dorian's character, and therefore causes the first visible change in his portrait. He considers the aesthetic pain caused by her poor acting to be on par with Sybil's emotional devastation at his rejection. This belief is rooted in the sentiment expressed by Lord Henry before the trio leaves for the play, when he says "I love acting. It is so much more real than life." This statement is a clear indication of Henry's continuing influence on Dorian.

We are also reminded of the statement in the preface that "Those who go beneath the surface [of art] do so at their peril." Dorian is not prepared to see the person beneath the surface of Sybil's acting. The preface also states that "It is the spectator, and not life, that art really mirrors." Dorian saw himself reflected in Sybil's acting, because it was artful, but once her acting is revealed as artless, he can no longer see himself in it, and his feelings for her disappear. What he thought was love for Sybil is really a form of vanity; the pain of enduring her poor performance is actually the pain of not seeing his own reflection.

In Chapter 7, Dorian undergoes several dramatic changes of character: he transforms from a devoted lover, to a bitter art critic, to a cruel betrayer, and seemingly back to a devoted lover. This final change is, however, superficial. He decides to do the honorable thing and marry Sybil, but only when faced with the possibility of watching the beautiful image in the portrait succumb to degradation. The corruption of Dorian's soul has begun in earnest, as reflected by the first visible change in the portrait.

Interestingly, this chapter marks a turning point in the narrative: the focus switches from Lord Henry to Dorian. Now that Henry's influence has begun to show its effects, the narrative no longer appears as concerned with Lord Henry himself. At this point, the story begins to focus solely on Dorian as a corrupt figure. At the end of the chapter, as Dorian feebly resolves to spend less time with Lord Henry and to marry Sybil, he is acting more out of vanity than out of love or a true sense of morality; a fact that will be revealed when the portrait fails to change for the better. This is not the last time Dorian will fail to recognize the vanity that lies behind his decisions.

Summary and Analysis of Chapter 8

Summary

Dorian is awoken by Victor, his servant, after having slept until 1:15 in the afternoon. He sees that he has received a letter from Lord Henry, but leaves it unopened. He feels refreshed and eats breakfast happily, the previous night feeling like nothing more than a dream. His pleasant afternoon is interrupted, however, when he sees the screen that he has thrown over the portrait. He thinks himself foolish for imagining that the painting might have changed, but decides to check it again just to make sure. Nervous that he might be acting strangely, he throws Victor out of the room, locks all of the doors, and draws the curtains. Sure enough, "It was perfectly true. The painting had altered." He wonders how this could possible, whether there is a scientific explanation, or a darker, metaphysical cause for the change. The cruel expression on the face in the portrait reminds him of his poor treatment of Sybil. Stricken with guilt, Dorian writes her a passionate love letter, filling "page after page with wild words of sorrow and wilder words of pain."

Writing the letter is deeply cathartic. As soon as he finishes, Lord Henry arrives. Dorian tells him that although he saw Sybil and was brutal towards her, he doesn't regret any of it, since "It has taught me how to know myself better." Henry is delighted to find Dorian in good spirits, but when the young man tells him that he plans to cleanse his soul by marrying the poor actress, it is clear that there has been a misunderstanding. Sybil Vane, as Henry had written to Dorian in the unopened letter, has killed herself with poison.

Henry says that there will be an inquest, but that Dorian has nothing to worry about since nobody saw him go backstage or leave the theater, and since Sybil never even told anyone her fiancé's real name. Henry urges Dorian not to get involved with the situation, as such a scandal would destroy his reputation. He asks Dorian to come see the opera with him that night. After his initial shock passes, Dorian responds to the news of Sybil's death with a strange detachment. "So I have murdered Sybil Vane," he thinks, "as surely as if I had cut her little throat with a knife. Yet the roses are not less lovely for all that."

Under Henry's direction, Dorian comes to appreciate Sybil's death as "a wonderful ending to a wonderful play." Dorian is briefly disturbed by his emotional detachment, but Henry soon assuages his guilt, saying that life's tragedies often "hurt us by...their entire lack of style." Since Sybil died so dramatically, and for such a pure purpose as love, the situation is actually one, Henry believes, that Dorian should take satisfaction and pleasure in. Henry goes so far as to state that since the girl was only ever alive on stage, and since Dorian's love for her was rooted in his admiration for the various heroines she portrayed, that "The girl never really lived, and so she has never really died...don't waste your tears over Sybil Vane. She was less real than [Shakespeare's characters] are." Dorian thanks Henry for being such a good and true friend.

Henry leaves, and Dorian again looks at the picture. The mean sneer has not shifted, making Dorian think that it had "received the news of Sybil Vane's death before he had known of it himself." After further contemplation, Dorian consoles himself by thinking that since the picture displays his true character, it must "bear the burden of his shame," thus leaving him to enjoy a guilt–free life. He sees no reason to consider *why* the picture changes, and decides to allow himself to simply be entertained by its progress. The chapter ends with Dorian leaving to meet Lord Henry at the opera.

Analysis

Once again, Dorian displays alarming capriciousness and a disturbing blindness to his own vanity. He writes to Sybil in a passion, taking all of the blame for his actions, but the narrator comments that "there is a luxury in self–reproach." He takes pleasure in his confession, privately praising his own "selflessness". He falls into a brief spell of grief upon hearing the news of Sybil's suicide, but proves to be far from inconsolable. Lord Henry, playing the devil to Dorian's Faust, shows him the means by which to transform his pain and guilt into a new, pleasurable experience, for which only the portrait will pay the price.

In this chapter, the symbolic significance of the portrait is clearly spelled out for us: "here was a visible symbol of the degradation of sin…an ever present sign of the ruin men bring upon their souls." This realization prompts Dorian to exclaim that he "can't bear the idea of my soul being hideous." Dorian fears physical ugliness; in other words, it is vanity, not morality, that defines Dorian's relationship with his soul. A similar type of selfishness appears when Dorian writes his love letter to Sybil. We are told that "There is a luxury in self–reproach…When Dorian had finished the letter, he felt that he had been forgiven." Even in the throes of guilt, Dorian does not need Sybil to grant the forgiveness that only she can rightly give, nor does it occur to him that Sybil would do anything other than immediately accept his apology and agree to be his wife.

Dorian's comment that Sybil's death seems "to be like simply a wonderful ending to a wonderful play" continues the theme of life imitating art. It also recalls Dorian's obsession with the characters that Sybil portrayed. He became disappointed in her when she tried to be her own person, and rejected the falseness of playing a role. Now, her death has given Dorian the ability to once again view Sybil as a character in a play. When Lord Henry encourages this interpretation of the tragedy, he ensures that Dorian passes the point of no return on his descent into immorality.

Dorian's statement that he has "murdered her…as if I had cut her little throat with a knife" not only displays a disturbing tendency to relish in unnecessarily morbid details, but also foreshadows Basil's murder in chapter 13, and recalls Basil's threat to destroy the painting with a knife in chapter 2. The image of death by stabbing hovers in the air throughout the novel.

This chapter also contains the closest thing Wilde offers as to an explanation of how the portrait has acquired such metaphysical properties. However, it is not actually an explanation at all, but merely idle conjecture from Dorian: "Was there some subtle affinity between the chemical atoms, that shaped themselves into form and colour on the canvas, and the soul that was within him? Could it be that what the soul thought, they realized? – that what it dreamed, they made true? Or was there some other, darker reason?" Dorian is briefly disturbed by the possibility that black magic is at work, but he soon shrugs off this fear, and the question of how and why the portrait changes is never again raised.

Summary and Analysis of Chapters 9 &10

Summary

The next day, Basil visits Dorian and is shocked to learn that he has been to the opera, given the circumstances. He is also aghast at the fact that Dorian seems altogether unmoved by Sybil's suicide. Dorian defends himself by telling Basil that "She passed again into the sphere of art. There is something of the martyr about her." He accuses Basil of being selfish, since his anger stems from the fact that he was not the one who consoled him, and tells the artist to "teach me to forget what has happened, or to see it from a proper artistic point of view."

Dorian does, however, admit to being strongly influenced by Lord Henry. He also admits that he knows Basil to be a much better man than Henry. When the painter hears this, his old affection for Dorian wins him over. He inquires whether Dorian has been summoned by the police. Dorian is annoyed by this thought, but assures Basil that no one involved even knows his name. He asks Basil to make him a drawing of Sybil, but Basil asks Dorian to instead come pose for him again – a request that is quickly denied.

Basil then notices that his painting is covered. When he asks to see his work, Dorian threatens never to speak to him again if he tries to lift the covering screen. He is determined never to share the secret of the painting with anyone. Basil says that he wants to exhibit the work, since he considers it his masterpiece, but Dorian states that that is also out of the question. The painter asks if Dorian has seen anything strange in the picture to disturb him so much. Thinking that Basil may already know about the picture's enchantment, Dorian says that he has, but asks his friend to explain himself. Basil confesses his idolatry of Dorian, and says that he was struck by how much of it had come across in the painting. Dorian is disappointed and unmoved by the painter's affection. He again states that he will never again sit for another portrait. Basil cries out that Dorian's refusal will "spoil my life as an artist" and leaves. Dorian, growing ever more paranoid and determined to conceal his secret, decides to hide the painting more thoroughly.

Dorian acquires the key to his attic from his housekeeper. Victor informs him that the men he has requested have arrived to help transport the painting, and Dorian sends his servant off to Lord Henry with a request for reading material. Mr Hubbard, a renowned frame–maker, and his assistants carry the portrait up to the attic without removing the cover, as per Dorian's instructions. Dorian wonders about the possibility of ever displaying the work, since it is Basil's masterpiece, but knows that even though "It might escape the hideousness of sin, the hideousness of age was in store for it." It would have to be hidden from sight forever so that "No eye but his would ever see his shame."

Once Mr Hubbard leaves, Dorian returns to his library to find a note from Lord

Henry, along with a newspaper clipping and an old, yellow book. A red mark on the newspaper brings Dorian's attention to a small article informing him that the inquest into Sybil's death has ruled it a certain suicide. He is free of suspicion. He begins reading the novel sent by Henry, a book about a young Parisian "who spent his life trying to realize…all the passions and modes of thought that belonged to every century except his own." He is so engrossed with the novel and its "metaphors as monstrous as orchids, and as subtle in color" that he is several hours late for his engagement with Lord Henry.

Analysis

Dorian defends himself for failing to mourn Sybil's death with a Lord Henry–ism: "A man who is master of himself can end sorrow as easily as he can invent a pleasure." The irony of claiming to be master of one's self by voicing the views of another escapes the young man, but serves to portray him as a deeply misguided soul. In Basil's confession to Dorian, he echoes several sentiments from the preface, saying that "what art should be [is] unconscious, ideal, and remote…Art is always more abstract than we fancy. Form and colour tell us of form and colour…art conceals the artist far more completely than it ever reveals him." These sentiments, although they are presented by Wilde as truths in the preface, are disheartening revelations for the painter. Basil had been hoping that the picture would show Dorian the truth about his affections, but when Dorian hears Basil's confession, he practically scoffs at it, and states aloud that he wonders if he will ever know such feelings of adoration. The answer (which Dorian himself is unaware of) is, of course, that he already adores himself in a nearly identical fashion. Later, when faced with further evidence of his own degradation, Dorian will blame himself for not accepting Basil's "pure, Uranian" love. This sentiment is one of the many homosexual references that remains in the novel after Wilde's revision of the *Lippincott* version. Wilde is said to have espoused the notion that love between two men was inherently purer and nobler than heterosexual love, and this sentiment appears briefly in Dorian's thoughts.

Concealing the picture is a clear symbolic gesture for Dorian's denial of his own shame. Since the painting is destined to display "the hideous corruption of his soul" while his face will remain young and innocent, Dorian believes that he can effectively live without the hindrance of a conscience so long as no one sees the painting. The downside of Dorian's obsession with his appearance, however, has already begun to show. He becomes suspicious of his housekeeper and of Victor, his servant, feeling sure that they will try to look at the picture. This paranoia can be seen as a principal stage in the protagonist's degrdation, an indication that the deterioration of Dorian's soul is well underway.

The attic where Dorian hides the painting was "a playroom when he was a child" and "a study when he grew somewhat older." The room is already a vault hiding his past, and it will now hide the degradation of his conscience, as well. This room becomes a symbol of the purity of youth and concern for morality that Dorian consciously rejects. Instead of skeletons in his closet, Dorian has a painting in his attic.

Some critics have interpreted the hidden painting as a metaphor for sexuality – Dorian keeps his shame and guilt about his homosexual tendencies "in the closet", as it were. While such a reading is compelling, it also over–simplifies Dorian's dilemma, while inadvertently assuming that Wilde would himself condemn homosexual tendencies. Dishonesty, betrayal, and murder all cause the portrait to wither, age, and grow more hideous. To assume that homosexual actions also deface the portrait is to present such actions as similarly offensive or reprehensible – a notion with which the author would have certainly disagreed.

Summary and Analysis of Chapter 11

Summary

Over the next several years, Dorian becomes obsessed with the book given to him by Lord Henry. He buys multiple copies of the "first edition, and [has] them bound in different colors so that they might suit his moods." To Dorian, "the whole book…seemed to contain the story of his own life, written before he had lived it." Like the book's young hero, Dorian begins immersing himself in varied interests, including religion, mysticism, music, jewels, ancient tapestries, and the study of his own ancestors. Dorian is, however, quick to change obsessions once they no longer interest him, following the whims of his desire with the passion of an artist. He clings to each current obsession fervently, studying it and acquiring as many fanciful examples of it as he can find. He buys extravagent gowns covered in hundreds of pearls to feed his interest in jewels, and ancient, golden–threaded tapestries to nourish his curiosity about embroidery. As soon as a given subject has exhausted itself in his mind, however, he drops it in favor of his next interest. For the next 18 years, capriciousness is a way of life for Dorian. In fact, Dorian's attitude recalls Lord Henry's own: "certainly, to him, Life itself was the first, the greatest, of the arts." No matter how intensely Dorian embraces a subject, "no theory of life seemed to him to be of any importance compared with life itself. He felt keenly conscious of how barren all intellectual speculation is when separated from action and experiment."

Dorian's "experiments" are often social in nature. He becomes notorious among London's aristocratic circles as a trend–setter, wearing the latest fashions and looked to as a judge of tastefulness. Young men emulate him, and young women are drawn to him. Those whom he befriends, however, are often ruined, and Dorian is eventually disdained as much as he is admired. Lord Henry seems to be the only close friend who sticks by Dorian over the years. Gossip begins following Dorian wherever he goes, and he becomes infamous, even despicable, in some social circles. He does, however, remain as attractive and fashionable as ever, and continues to be admired for his exquisite taste. No matter how poorly people speak of him, his youthful beauty and the boyish innocence of his face never fail to win him new friends.

Dorian also takes to making periodic visits to the attic to watch the painting transform, "wondering sometimes which were the more horrible, the signs of sin or the signs of age." At first, as the painting grows uglier, Dorian becomes "more and more enamored of his own beauty, more and more interested in the corruption of his soul." He even begins to mock the portrait. Over time, however, his various obsessions and social excursions become ways for him to escape what he knows to be the truth of his soul.

Analysis

This chapter initiates the second half of the novel, in which Lord Henry's influence has fully bloomed and Dorian has become his own person, with his own interests, convictions, and notoriety amongst London's aristocracy. After this chapter, the protagonist is no longer a corruptable youth, and is rather a full–fledged corruptor in his own right. We learn that Dorian's personality, charming as it may be, is defined by capriciousness, and a passion for new pleasures.

Dorian's obsession with Lord Henry's book may be interpreted in a number of different ways. The plot reminds him of his own life; the hero reminds him of himself. The narrator mentions "the latter part of the book, with its really tragic…account of the sorrow and despair of one who had himself lost what in others, and in the world, he most dearly valued." This is a fitting description for the end of *Dorian Gray*, as well. The question remains, however, of whether the book happens to describe Dorian's character, or whether Dorian is changing to mimic the book's protagonist. Once again, Wilde is blurring the distinction between life and art.

Indeed, we learn in this chapter that for Dorian, life and art are interchangeable. Like Lord Henry, he considers pleasure and aesthetic value more important than anything else. To him, any new and pleasurable experience is worth having, even if that experience is hurtful to others. The chapter closes with the statement that "There were moments when he looked on evil simply as a mode through which he could realize his conception of the beautiful." In these moments, Dorian is the most degraded, and his soul suffers the most disfiguration.

Dorian reaches a point where he can only be happy when he forgets about the picture in his attic. He manages to avoid facing it for weeks at a time, but like any addict, he can't force himself to stay away from it for very long. The corruption of his soul torments him, and he escapes that torment by indulging in vices that aggravate his corruption and torment him further. This vicious cycle consciously mimics the patterns of withdrawal and greater dependence commonly faced by drug addicts, an analogy that becomes much more explicit in later chapters, when we learn of Dorian's dependence on opium.

The struggle to deny the nagging guilt he feels when faced with the portrait lies beneath all of Dorian's actions, which brings the nature of his fervent passion for his capricious endeavors into question. Is he naturally such a passionate person, or does his passion spring from a desperate need to occupy his mind with anything other than the undeniable and monstrous corruption of his soul?

Summary and Analysis of Chapters 12 &13

Summary

Late one night, Dorian runs into Basil Hallward on the street. Basil is delighted to see him, as he has been searching for Dorian all night, wanting to say goodbye before leaving on a six month trip to Paris. Basil has several hours before his train leaves, and the two adjourn to Dorian's home. The painter tells Dorian that he has been worried because "the most dreadful things are being said against [him] in London." Dorian is annoyed, and tells his friend that he doesn't care for gossip, but makes no effort to defend himself. Disconcerted by his friend's apathy, Basil goes on to assure Dorian that, vicious and damning as many of the rumors are, he doesn't believe them because he trusts that Dorian is a good person, and that "sin is a thing that writes itself across a man's face. It cannot be concealed." Dorian looks as young and innocent as ever, and Basil believes his eyes.

Once the artist begins listing the names of people whom Dorian is said to have led astray, Dorian rebukes him, saying that he doesn't know what he's talking about, and warning him to mind his own business. He argues that no person is without sin or temptation, and that corruption is not a thing that can be taught. Dorian only feels responsible for showing people their true selves. During their discussion, Basil remarks that he feels as if he doesn't know Dorian at all, and that in order to know him "I should have to see your soul." This sends Dorian into an odd state of defensive paranoia. Laughing, he tells Basil that "You shall see [my soul] yourself tonight!" Basil is confused and frightened by Dorian's words. He wants his friend to deny the charges against him, and is unsure whether Dorian's refusal to do so amounts to an admission that they are, in fact, true. To answer all of Basil's doubts, Dorian invites the painter upstairs, to view his "diary".

They ascend the stairs in Dorian's house, and enter the attic. Dorian tells Basil to open the curtain if he wishes to see his soul. Basil, thinking his friend is mad, hesitates, and Dorian reveals the painting himself. The artist is horrified, and at first doesn't even recognize Dorian in "the hideous face on the canvas grinning at him." He refuses to believe that it's actually his own painting, thinking it to be some "foul parody," until he recognizes the frame, and finds his own signature at the bottom. Dorian observes Basil's horrified reaction with apathy, and reminds him of the wish he made years ago at the painter's studio, right after the portrait had been completed. Basil is overwhelmed by disgust, unsure of what to believe, and exclaims that Dorian must have been a devil all along, and that if this picture accurately reflects the man's soul, that he "must be worse even than those who talk against you fancy you to be!"

He urges Dorian to repent, to try and save his soul, at which point "an uncontrollable feeling of hatred for Basil Hallward came over him, as though it had been suggested to him by the image on the canvas, whispered into his ear by those grinning lips." In a frenzy, Dorian grabs a knife and plunges it into Basil's neck, stabbing him repeatedly, and then holds him down until he stops struggling and dies, a pool of blood spreading out across the table and weaving through the feet of his chair.

Dorian is surprised at the ease with which he performed the murder. He feels relieved by the thought that the man "who had painted the fatal portrait to which all his misery had been due, had gone out of his life." He leaves the attic and determines that he will be able to get away with his crime, since Basil was supposed to leave for Paris that night, and since no one knew of his visit. He will destroy Basil's bag and overcoat, but in order to get rid of the body, he must call on Alan Campbell.

Analysis

Basil speaks at length about Dorian's alleged sins, but never actually states what these sins are, only saying that Dorian's "name was implicated in the most terrible confession I'd ever read." This propensity for only indirectly acknowledging the breaking of social taboos is an interesting tendency found in Victorian society, one shared by the narrator of *Dorian Gray*. We have read that there are rumors of Dorian's misdeeds but unless we witness them first–hand, as we do the murder, we never learn what they actually are. Like Basil, we can only assume the worst, based on the hideousness of the portrait.

That Wilde chooses to portray Dorian's transgressions in such a manner is worth noting. The narrator is clearly omniscient: he certainly appears capable of informing us about what, exactly, Dorian has done to spark so much gossip and disdain, but by only hinting at the nature of Dorian's transgressions, Wilde establishes a palpable sense of their illicitness, leading the reader to look for clues while also reinforcing the sense of Dorian's degradation.

Basil's condemnation of Dorian's sins, and his fervent desire for Dorian to repent, indicate a religiosity in the artist that was absent in our last encounter with him. Basil has acquired a sharply refined ethical sensibility. This may explain the decline in his artistic output, since Wilde states in the preface that "An ethical sympathy in an artist is an unpardonable mannerism of style." This "unpardonable mannerism" is partially responsible for Dorian's murderous rage, as it offends his artistic sensibility, which is the only claim to purity that he now feels justified in clinging to. We are, however, told that the murder is prompted most directly by the portrait itself: "an uncontrollable feeling of hatred…came over him, as though it had been suggested to him by the image on the canvas." The image confronts Dorian with his shameful life, and Dorian blames Basil, the painter, for the pain that he feels.

When the artist confronts Dorian, it is too much for him to bear, and he is driven to murder by "the mad passions of a hunted animal." Ever since he first encountered Lord Henry, Dorian has made a point of surrendering to his passions. Now, even the urge towards murderous violence cannot be checked. Try as he might in later chapters, he is never able to write off this crime as simply another new and exciting "artistic" experience, as he was able to do with Sybil's death.

Violent images involving knives are found in several instances throughout the novel: in addition to Basil's murder, they are found when Basil threatens to destroy the portrait in chapter 2, and when Dorian reflects that he has killed Sybil as if he had "cut her little throat with a knife" in chapter 8.

Summary and Analysis of Chapter 14

Summary

Dorian awakes from a dreamless sleep and gradually remembers the terrible events of the previous night. He writes a letter summoning Alan Campbell, and sends his servant to deliver it. While he is waiting, he distracts himself from his guilt by reading poetry from a book given to him by a man named Adrian Singleton, and reflects on the course of his friendship with Alan Campbell.

The two men first met at a party. Alan was a man of science, a chemist, but the two initially bonded over their shared love of music. Alan "was an extremely clever young man," but "whatever little sense of the beauty of poetry he possessed he had gained entirely from Dorian." For a while the two were inseparable, but for unspecified reasons Alan began leaving parties whenever Dorian showed up and refusing to speak with him or interact with him in any way. Alan withdrew from society almost entirely, immersing himself in his experiments.

The long wait nags at Dorian, but Alan eventually arrives. Dorian speaks cordially, but his guest is cold, curt, and suspicious of his host's motives. Cutting to the chase, Dorian tells him that he needs him to get rid of a dead body, the result of a suicide. Alan refuses and wants nothing to do with the situation – or with Dorian at all, for that matter. Dorian, hoping to win Alan's sympathy, confesses that it was murder, and says that he only needs Alan to pretend to carry out an experiment. It becomes clear that Alan is determined to resist all of Dorian's tactics.

Reluctantly, Dorian turns to blackmail, showing him a letter that he promises to send unless the scientist agrees to help. Alan succumbs to "the disgrace with which he was threatened," and writes a letter for his assistant, detailing the tools to be brought at once to Dorian's house. The tools are delivered, and Dorian dismisses his servant for the evening so that he does not become suspicious.

The two men haul the heavy trunk of tools upstairs. Dorian realizes that for the first time he has forgotten to cover the painting before leaving the attic. He rushes to throw the curtain over it, but before he does so he notices the sickening gleam of red blood on the hands of his doppelganger. Alan arrives with the trunk, locks himself in the attic, and goes to work. Around seven in the evening, the deed is done. Basil's body has been incinerated, and Alan leaves with the words "Let us never see each other again."

Analysis

Until now, we have heard the names Alan Campbell and Adrian Singleton mentioned on the list of names of those Dorian has corrupted, but this chapter contains the first instance of a face–to–face interaction with one of them. Aside from Sybil, these two are the only people whose lives Dorian has ruined who actually appear in the book. Once again, the narrator refuses to state the reasons for the bitterness Alan displays towards Dorian, or the content of Dorian's blackmail letter, but these omissions only heighten our sense of how allegedly unspeakable their transgressions must have been. We learn that Alan no longer wishes to show his face in public, and we have learned in earlier chapters that Adrian is likewise ostracized. The likeliest causes for this shame – homosexual encounters – are, however, only tacitly present.

When Wilde himself stood trial for accusations of sodomy in the years following this book's publication, he wrote of "the note of doom that…runs through…*Dorian Gray*"; it was instances such as these that Wilde was referring to. Wilde revised later editions of the book in an effort to reduce the prominence of the homosexual undertones, but they were too integral an aspect of the interactions between the main characters to be eliminated entirely.

Dorian's cordiality towards Alan when his guest first arrives is a facade. His seeming reluctance to blackmail the man is insincere, an indication that Dorian actually takes pleasure from the manipulative power he holds over Alan. Alan is not fooled by Dorian's pretense of kindness, but has no choice but to comply with his wishes. In this interaction, we witness how refined Dorian's capacity for social persuasion has become during the 18 years glossed over in chapter 11. He has been a good student of Lord Henry, now equalling, or parhaps surpassing, the older man's powers of manipulation.

The poem that Dorian reads while waiting for Alan is significant for several reasons. First, it is from a book given to him by Adrian Singleton. Dorian relies on the gift of a man that he has somehow betrayed for comfort. The lines that he repeats over and over to himself, "Devant une facade rose/ Sur le marbre d'un escalier," are translated as "Upon a red–faced town/ On the marble of a stairway." These lines seem to encapsulate Venice for Dorian, who has visited the city with Basil. Remembering the painter, however, only leads him to remark "Poor Basil! What a horrible way to die!" Dorian is unwilling to openly admit that he is directly responsibile for Basil's death. In fact, Dorian instead blames Basil for the suffering caused by the painting. This is, of course, highly delusional behavior. It would make more sense to blame Lord Henry, his corruptor, but even this would be inaccurate. Dorian himself is responsible for wishing the enchantment into existence. However, the genuine acceptance of responsibility for his misdeeds is well beyond Dorian's ethical capacities at this point.

Summary and Analysis of Chapter 14

Summary and Analysis of Chapters 15 &16

Summary

Later that evening, Dorian attends a party thrown by Lady Narborough, a wealthy widow and popular socialite. He acts naturally and comfortably, charming his hostess and successfully masking his tortured conscience, but is unable to stomach any food. Most of the guests are dull and witless, so Dorian is glad when Lord Henry arrives. As usual, Dorian delights in Henry's paradoxical, slightly offensive witticisms. The evening goes smoothly until Dorian is asked how he spent the previous night. He founders and retracts several answers, clearly discombobulated and unnecessarily defensive. Henry can easily see that something is wrong, but when he tries to get Dorian to share his troubles, the younger man excuses himself, saying that he is "out of temper" and "must go home."

Once home, Dorian faces the fact that Basil's belongings, which he had left in Dorian's closet, still have to be destroyed. He throws them into his fireplace, feeling sick at the smell of burning fabric and leather. He is then overcome by an unspecified "mad craving." He examines "a small Chinese box of black and gold–dust lacquer" taken from one of his cabinets, and decides to leave. His cab driver at first refuses to take him where he wants to go, but soon relents and accepts Dorian's bribe.

During the long cab ride, Dorian remembers Lord Henry's words from their first meeting: "To cure the soul by means of the senses, and the senses by means of the soul." He feels as if his soul is quite sick, and takes comfort in the idea of curing it. He dismounts from the cab and walks several blocks, nervously checking behind him, until he finds a small, dilapidated house hidden in an alley between two factories.

He enters the house, which is revealed to be an opium den. Inside are groups of haggard, complacent, disheveled individuals. Among them is Adrian Singleton, who joins Dorian at the bar. They are harassed by two women, and Dorian walks out of the place. As he is leaving, one of the women calls him "Prince Charming," at which point an unrecognized sailor springs to his feet and pursues Dorian outside. The sailor grabs Dorian by the throat, brings him to his knees, and points a revolver in his face, telling him that he is the brother of Sybil Vane, whom Dorian drove to suicide. He only knew his sister's lover by the nickname "Prince Charming." Dorian pretends to have never heard of Sybil Vane, and tells James to hold his face under the lamplight. James complies, and realizes that he has made a mistake: Sybil died 18 years ago, making her lover nearly 40, but the person standing before him looks no older than 20. James is embarrassed, and begs Dorian's forgiveness. Dorian chides him for his behavior and flees.

James then speaks with the two women from the bar and learns that Dorian is much older than he seems. One of the women remarks that "it's nigh on eighteen year since Prince Charming made me what I am." Realizing that he has been deceived, James rushes after Dorian in an outrage, but turns the corner to find that the villain has already disappeared.

Analysis

Dorian succumbs to paranoia at Lady Narborough's home, but his fear of being discovered prove unnecessary. His hostess tells him that "you are made to be good – you look so good." The inability to accept the possibility that a young, innocent appearance hides anything other than an innocent, beautiful personality is a common one in Dorian's social circle; this superficiality is what allows him to maintain a level of respect and admiration, despite the preponderance of nasty rumors, and even despite the guilt of a murder weighing on his conscience.

Wilde uses Dorian's group of friends to parody the superficiality of London's aristocracy. Lord Henry's convictions that beauty is the most important thing in the world and that physical beauty is the greatest asset a person can have seem to be shockingly accurate, at least amongst people such as those whom Dorian and Henry associate with. This raises an important question: if Lord Henry's morally shallow beliefs are justified, can we condemn his character for espousing them?

Dorian's odd mannerisms while handling the ornate box of opium and his discreet flight to the opium den reveal an addiction that we have been thus far unaware of. Dorian has always escaped his guilt by immersing himself in pleasurable distractions, but his lapse into addiction signifies that he has sunk to yet a lower level of degradation. This addiction also reminds us of the nature of Dorian's relationship to the portrait. Like an addict, Dorian cannot refrain from seeking out and indulging himself in new guilty pleasures. And, like an addict, Dorian cannot help but return to the attic and bask in the horror of his disfigured soul.

Adrian's presence in the opium den bothers Dorian because he "wanted to be where no one knew who he was. He wanted to escape from himself." His past, however, haunts him no matter where he turns. One might expect Dorian to take some solace from the fact that, unlike Alan Campbell, Adrian is willing to interact with Dorian, but other people mean so little to Dorian at this point that he can only view Adrian as a nuisance. Instead of taking pity on Adrian's deplorable state, Dorian is repulsed.

The inescapability of the past is also exemplified by the reappearance of Sybil's vengeful brother. James Vane seeks revenge for the very first instance of Dorian's corruption: the act of selfish vanity that caused the initial change in the painting. James's determination to avenge his sister's death represents the culmination of all of Dorian's sins, returning to hunt him down. However, superficiality does not fail Dorian yet; in this first encounter with James, Dorian's face literally saves his life.

Summary and Analysis of Chapters 17 &18

Summary

The chapter begins with Dorian and Lord Henry chatting with Gladys, the Duchess of Monmouth, during a party at a conservatory. Many guests are gathered there for an extended visit as guests of Dorian's. The guests discuss names, love, and of course the virtues of beauty. Gladys shows herself to be quite witty, holding her own in a tete–a–tete with Lord Henry. After Henry playfully mentions Dorian's old nickname, Prince Charming, she asks whether Dorian has ever truly been in love. Disturbed by the reminder of his recent confrontation, Dorian excuses himself, saying that he must pick orchids for the duchess.

Dorian takes a long time to return, and as Henry wonders about his whereabouts, a disturbed cry is heard from the other room. Lord Henry rushes to the scene, and finds that Dorian has fainted. Henry insists that he stay in bed and recover, but Dorian doesn't want to be alone. All of the guests assume that he has merely collapsed from exhaustion. Dorian, however, doesn't tell them the real reason for his distress: he fainted upon seeing the face of James Vane, spying on him through the conservatory window.

Dorian spends the next three days inside, "sick with a wild terror of dying, and yet indifferent to life itself." He eventually convinces himself that the face was a hallucination brought on by his conscience as a result of suppressing his guilt for so long. When Dorian finally goes outdoors, he and Lord Henry accompany Sir Geoffrey Clouston, the duchess's brother, on a short hunting excursion. Geoffrey aims at a hare, and Dorian instinctively cries out, urging him not to shoot it. Two screams are heard after the shot is fired: "the cry of a hare in pain, which is dreadful," and "the cry of a man in agony, which is worse." Geoffrey assumes that the man he has shot is a "beater," one of the men employed by the conservatory to drive the game into the open for the hunters.

All hunting is called off for the day, so that the guests don't appear too callous, and Lord Henry informs Geoffrey that the man who has been shot is dead. Later, Henry and Dorian again chat with Gladys. We learn that Geoffrey is upset, but Henry blames the beater for everything and sees no reason for any remorse. He wishes, however, "that he had done the thing on purpose," and proclaims that "I should like to know someone who had committed a real murder." Dorian must excuse himself to lie down.

He lies on a sofa upstairs, terrified, feeling as if the unexpected stranger's death is a sure sign that his own is imminent. He is nearly paralyzed with fear and decides to leave for a doctor, but before he can his valet sends the gamekeeper in. Knowing it must be about the dead beater, Dorian questions whether the victim had had a wife or any dependents, and offers "any sum of money you may think necessary" to provide for their needs. However, the gamekeeper has arrived to inform Dorian that the dead man was not an employee, and that no one has been able to identify him. Dorian frantically rides to the farm house where the body is being kept, and discovers that the dead man is James Vane. He is overjoyed, his eyes "full of tears, for he knew he was safe."

Analysis

The discussion of names and Henry's comment that "I never quarrel with actions [but] with words" prompt us to consider the significance of names in the novel, and the theme of the power of words. Upon first meeting Lord Henry in chapter 2, and first hearing the man's intoxicatingly sensuous view of the world, Dorian thinks to himself: "Words! Mere words! How terrible they were!...One could not escape from them." It is Henry's conversational acumen that enables him to influence Dorian so profoundly, and it is a book (Henry's gift, which Dorian obsesses over in chapter 11) that Dorian considers to be primarily responsible for his own corruption.

By placing such emphasis on the power of words, written or spoken, Wilde is indirectly commenting on the power of the literary art. Fittingly, Henry follows his earlier comment with the remark, "That is the reason I hate vulgar realism in literature." This comment is not merely an expression of yet another of Henry's distinctive beliefs, but an invitation for the reader to consider the value of the fantastic elements included in *The Picture of Dorian Gray*.

The Duchess of Monmouth is one of the few characters in the book who seems capable of holding her own in conversation against Lord Henry's sharp, unorthodox witticisms. When she says to Henry that "You value beauty far too much," she unknowingly hits on the reason for Dorian's guilt. When Dorian leaves to pick flowers, we are reminded of the first chapter, when Henry picked a flower from Basil's garden and slowly pulled it apart, petal by petal. As Henry's earlier action symbolized his role as both an admirer and a destroyer of delicate beauty, Dorian's action reveals that he has now symbolically replaced his mentor in this way as well.

The insensitivity of the party–goers upon hearing that a man has been shot is so extreme that it reads as a parody. Sir Geoffrey's first response upon learning that he has shot a man is annoyance; he says that the event "spoiled my shooting for the day." Lord Henry handles the news with typically superficial concern, saying that hunting must cease for the day because "It would not look well to go on." For all of the seeming profundity of the sayings that Henry spouts in conversation, he proves himself to be, in times of crisis, incapable of viewing the world in terms of anything but appearances. His comments in this chapter remind us of the superficial nature of his comfort to Dorian immediately after Sybil's death (chapter 8), when he recommended that Dorian not sulk or involve himself with the investigation so as to preserve his reputation.

Dorian himself displays some distress upon hearing of the man's death, but not for humanitarian reasons. He urges Sir Geoffrey not to shoot, but only because the intended target, a rabbit, strikes him as beautiful. Perhaps, since Dorian has felt like a hunted creature ever since his encounter with James Vane outside of the opium den, he sympathizes with the creature. The emotional pain Dorian feels after learning that a man is dead is the consequence of his own self–pity: he considers the event a "bad omen," not a tragedy in its own right. Dorian displays his true insensitivity when his immediate reaction to the news is to reach for his checkbook. He is not compelled to comfort the family of what he assumes to be a dead employee, or even to express his condolences, but rather instinctually attempts to make the problem go away by throwing money at it.

Discovering that the dead man is James Vane causes Dorian to rejoice for several reasons. First and foremost, he no longer has to fear for his life. However, it also means that he was not hallucinating when he saw James's face through the window. Dorian may be cripplingly paranoid, but he is not insane. Finally, since James's appearance was intended to make Dorian pay for his hand in Sybil's death, now that James is dead, Dorian may once again convince himself that he has escaped unscathed from the sins of his past.

Summary and Analysis of Chapter 19

Summary

Several months later, Dorian is back in London, conversing with Lord Henry at the older man's house. Dorian, it seems, has decided to change his ways. Henry tells him that he is perfect the way he is and that there's no use trying to change, but Dorian replies that "I have done too many dreadful things in my life," and that "I began my good actions yesterday." His so–called "good action" was his treatment of Hetty, a beautiful young peasant girl who reminded him of Sybil Vane. She fell in love with Dorian, but instead of taking advantage of her and breaking her heart, as was his usual way, he "determined to leave her as flower–like as [he] had found her."

Henry mocks him and asks whether he's sure that Hetty "isn't floating at the present moment in some star–lit millpond…like Ophelia." This upsets Dorian, as he desperately wants to believe in the value of his good intentions. The conversation turns towards the whereabouts of Basil Hallward. The painter's disappearance, now six weeks old, is still the talk of the town, along with Henry's divorce and the suicide of Alan Campbell. Henry asks Dorian to play Chopin for him, because "The man with whom my wife ran away played Chopin exquisitely."

At the piano, Dorian nonchalantly asks what Henry would think if he told him that he had murdered Basil. "I would say," he responds, "that you were posing for a character that didn't suit you." Such crimes, Henry believes, are the specialty of the lower classes. Besides, Henry cannot imagine that Basil would have met such a romantic end, because his paintings had steadily declined in the years following his soiled friendship with Dorian. His painting of Dorian was, apparently, his final masterpiece. Henry believes that the painting was stolen a long time ago, and Dorian claims to have forgotten all about it.

Henry catches Dorian off–guard by paraphrasing the Bible, asking him: "what does it profit a man if he gain the whole world and lose…his soul?" When Dorian is startled by this statement, Henry just laughs, telling him that he heard a preacher posing this quesiton to a crowd during a walk through the park on a rainy day. Henry describes his amusement at the spectacle of the somber crowd standing in the rain, listening to "an uncouth Christian in a macintosh." He apparently wanted to tell the preacher that "Art had a soul, but that man did not."

Henry's light–heartedness offends Dorian, who says that "The soul is a terrible reality…It can be poisoned or made perfect." He tells Henry that he is certain of this fact, to which Henry replies, "then it must be an illusion. The things one feels absolutely certain about are never true." Dorian begins to play a nocturne by Chopin, which greatly affects Henry and prompts a rambling tirade on romance and how exquisite Dorian's life has been. Dorian agrees, but reminds Henry that he has turned over a new leaf, and that he will never forgive him for his corrupting influence. On his way out, Henry invites Dorian to lunch the next day, and Dorian reluctantly agrees to accompany the older man.

Analysis

When telling Henry about Hetty, Dorian insists that she will "live, like Perdita, in her garden," to which Henry asks "how do you know that Hetty isn't floating…like Ophelia?" These are both Shakespearean characters (from *The Winter's Tale* and *Hamlet*, respectively) that Sybil used to play on stage. Dorian has already stated that Hetty reminds him of Sybil, whom he loved because of all the characters she represented to him. Dorian now seeks to make amends for his treatment of Sybil vicariously, through Hetty; he thinks of her as Perdita, a character who meets a happy ending. Lord Henry's allusion to the tragic character of Ophelia is unbearable to Dorian because it reminds him of the actual circumstances of Sybil's death, and his callous decision to view it as a theatrical drama.

Shakespeare is also evoked after Henry inquires about the state of Basil's painting. While playing the piano, Dorian says that the picture reminded him of certain lines from Hamlet: "Like the painting of a sorrow,/ A face without a heart." This lines relate directly and poignantly to Dorian's condition. They not only refer to the painting, but to Dorian himself, who now feels reduced to "a face without a heart." When Henry tires to coax Dorian out of his somber mood with the line "If a man treats life artistically, his brain is his heart", Dorian only repeats the quotation. It is if Dorian is trying to obliquely communicate his true plight to Henry. He has already attempted, albeit unsuccessfully, to confess to Basil's murder. Dorian is hopelessly isolated even from his oldest remaining friend. Before leaving to return home, Dorian hesitates at the door, "as if he had something more to say," but says nothing, a further indication of his pathetic lonliness.

Although Henry fancies himself to be Dorian's best friend, he tells Dorian that, after all their years together, "you are still the same." This reminds us that, for all of his seeming wisdom, Lord Henry can still only take things at face value; to him, looking the same and being the same are one and the same thing. He has no clue as to the true degradation of Dorian's character.

Henry's earlier comment that a man ought to "treat life artistically," one of the major themes of the book, is best considered in conjunction with the closing remark of the preface, that "All art is quite useless." Considering that this is the opinion of the author, it is clear that trying to make a work of art out of one's life will not be very rewarding in *Dorian Gray*.

Dorian remarks that Henry "poisoned me with a book once," and tells his friend to "promise me that you will never lend that book to anyone. It does harm." Dorian has done precisely what the preface warns against when it declares that "All art is…surface," and that "Those who go beneath the surface do so at their peril." He has gone so deeply "beneath the surface" of the book that he has transformed it into a sort of outline for his own life. The corruption of his soul, and the ruin of his life, is what this "peril" has wrought on Dorian.

Summary and Analysis of Chapter 20

Summary

During the walk home from Henry's, Dorian enjoys the warm evening. He is annoyed when several people mutter his name in astonishment as he passes, an occurence that used to please him, but he cheers himself by thinking of the beautiful and innocent Hetty, and his recent "good action." She had been hopelessly naive, but this was her charm, "she had everything that he had lost." He arrives at home and looks at his face in a mirror given to him by Henry long ago, but is so overcome with loathing that he shatters the mirror on the floor. He tries to focus on the future, to block out people like James Vane, now "hidden in a nameless grave," Alan Campbell, who shot himself without betraying Dorian's secret, or Basil Hallward, who Dorian "murdered in the madness of a moment." He attempts to assuage his guilt by blaming all of his troubles on Basil's portrait, and by contemplating the new life he has begun. He thinks of Hetty, the preservation of whose innocence he holds as proof of his newfound goodness, and wonders whether his good deed has caused his portrait to change for the better. He climbs to the attic, locks the door behind him, and throws the curtain from the picture.

A horrified gasp escapes his lips when he sees "no change, save that in the eyes there was a look of cunning, and in the mouth the curved wrinkle of the hypocrite." Dorian realizes that his kindness towards Hetty was either an act of vanity, driven by his desire to improve the appearance of his soul, or simply a different sort of selfishness, driven by "the desire for a new sensation." Desperate to escape his past crimes, Dorian sees the painting as the one piece of evidence revealing his guilt: "It had been like a conscience to him…He would destroy it." The knife on the table, he notices, is still stained with Basil's blood. He takes it, cleans it several times, and stabs the picture.

Dorian's servants are awoken by a dreadful shriek. It is so loud that two passing gentlemen hear it from the sidewalk and fetch a policeman to the house. The policeman informs them that it is Dorian Gray's residence, and the men walk away, sneering, without reporting the scream. The servants cannot open the locked door of the attic, so they manage to climb in through the roof. They find the body of a "withered, wrinkled, and loathsome" man, lying on the floor with a knife in his chest. They only recognize their master from the rings on his fingers.

Analysis

While thinking of Hetty, Dorian remembers telling her that he was a very wicked man, to which she responded that "wicked people were always very old and very ugly." Like the shallow people of Dorian's class, the "pure" Hetty assumes that appearance is everything. While this superficiality is precisely what allows Dorian to win so many hearts, it also prevents anyone from truly knowing who he is.

Dorian resolves to undo his past, to block it from his thoughts, and to focus on ensuring a positive future. He crushes the mirror given to him by Lord Henry, a symbolic rejection of his own vanity and the corrupting influence of Henry's friendship. He desperately clings to his treatment of Hetty as an indicator that it is possible to cleanse his soul, but it is too little, too late. Even this seemingly conscientious gesture was committed out of the hedonistic desire to experience an unfamiliar sensation, and the vain wish to improve the appearance of his soul, as depicted in the portrait. Vanity, not morality, drove his action, proving once again that Dorian is a condemned soul.

When Dorian kills himself by trying to destroy the painting, the picture and the man once again trade appearances. The man in the portrait becomes young and beautiful, while the real Dorian becomes old and disfigured by guilt. Dorian has unwittingly realized the fear he had upon first seeing the painting: that he would wither and die, while the painting would remain young and beautiful forever. Furthermore, since the painting has been restored to its original appearance, the masterpiece of Basil Hallward is returned to the world. Dorian, seeing the knife, thinks that "As it had killed the painter, so it would kill the painter's work" (177), but the work and the painter are instead granted the immortality of artistic greatness, while Dorian himself is destroyed.

The weapon used by Dorian is the same one he had used to kill Basil. Ironically, Basil offered to destroy the painting with a knife as soon as he sensed Dorian's negative reaction to it (chapter 2), but Dorian's newfound vanity and appreciation for artistic beauty prompted him to throw his own body in front of the image. Eighteen years and eighteen chapters later, Dorian decides to do precisely what he had prevented from happening, and once again his body throws itself before the painting, subject to the dangers of its beauty.

Suggested Essay Questions

1. In the preface, Wilde claims that there is "no such thing as a moral or an immoral book," and that an "ethical sympathy in an artist is an unpardonable mannerism of style." Yet Dorian's eventual ruin suggests a strong moral warning against the protagonist's vanity and selfishness. Is Wilde breaking his own rules and exhibiting "an unpardonable mannerism of style"? Or is the book meant to be read amorally?

2. Lord Henry and Dorian claim to be artists in the way they live their lives. Is this true, based on Wilde's definition of the artist, as expressed in the preface? Is this true based on your own definition?

3. Time moves linearly in *The Picture of Dorian Gray*, but not in even increments. Discuss the passage of time in the novel and how it influences our impression of characters and events. Be sure to touch on the glossing–over of 18 years in chapter 11.

4. When Basil confronts Dorian about the fact that he has allegedly corrupted many people, Dorian defends himself by saying that "Each of us has Heaven and Hell in him." Is Dorian responsible for the ruined lives of his friends? Is Lord Henry responsible for the ruined life of Dorian?

5. Dorian is outwardly young and charming, and inwardly old and corrupt. He is decidedly inconsistent in his social interactions and intellectal interests, while extremely consistent in appearance. Discuss the theme of duplicity throughout the novel.

6. In chapter 11, we encounter a peculiar first–person interjection from the narrator: "Is insincerity such a terrible thing? I think not." Does this voice, or this argument, remind you of any of the characters in the novel? Discuss Wilde's narrative voice in three or four instances. How does it relate to the different characters, does it seem to espouse similar views, or to sympathize with certain people more than others? Are we expected to trust the narrator on every occasion? What does this tell us about how the story is told?

7. At the time of its publication, *The Picture of Dorian Gray* sparked countless debates about the role of morality in art. What is your contribution to this debate? Do artists have the responsibility to convey good morals to their audience?

8. In 1895, the critic Ernest Newman, in a discussion of Wilde's contribution to literary thought, celebrated the author's use of paradoxes, saying that "a paradox is a truth seen round a corner" (Drew xxv). Countless paradoxes appear in *The Picture of Dorian Gray*, most often in the words of Lord Henry Wotton. Identify and discuss several paradoxes in the novel.

9. Traditionally, faustian tales contain explicit depictions of the protagonist's pact with the devil, giving a clearly defined source for his later woes. But the closest Wilde comes to identifying the reason for the portrait's metaphyisical powers is in chapter 8, when Dorian wonders if there is somehow "some subtle affinity between the chemical atoms, that shaped themselves into form and colour on the canvas, and the soul that was

within." Wilde seems content to leave the actual mechanism by which the portrait ages and withers instead of Dorian completely unexplained. How does this affect our overall impression of the novel? How would the work be different if it included, for instance, a scene in which Mephistofoles appears and has Dorian sign a contract?

Dorian Gray In Other Media

The Portrait of Dorian Gray has only grown in popularity throughout the 20th century. As a testament to this fact, there have been several notable film and stage adaptations of the book, as well as comic books featuring the character of Dorian. This picture shows the cover of the 1945 movie version, adapted from the novel and directed by Albert Lewin. It is faithful to the original work in many respects, but deviates mainly in its inclusion of an original character named Gladys Hallward, the niece of Basil Hallward, who becomes Dorian's primary love interest.

The character of Dorian Gray made its most recent cinematic appearance in 2003's *The League of Extraordinary Gentlemen*.

Author of ClassicNote and Sources

Jon Carter, author of ClassicNote. Completed on September 17, 2005, copyright held by GradeSaver.

Updated and revised Jordan Berkow December 06, 2005. Copyright held by GradeSaver.

Oscar Wilde. The Picture of Dorian Gray. Hertfordshire: Wordsworth, 2001.

John M. L. Drew. Introduction. The Picture of Dorian Gray. Hertfordshire: Wordsworth, 2001.

C. George Sandulescu (Ed.). Rediscovering Oscar Wilde. Gerrards Cross, England: Smythe, 1994.

Joseph Bristow, Oscar Wilde, Russell Jackson, Ian Small. The Complete Works Of Oscar Wilde: The Picture of Dorian Gray, The 1890 and 1891 Texts. Oxford: Oxford University Press, 2005.

Neil McKenna. The Secret Life of Oscar Wilde. New York: Basic Books, 2005.

"IMDb The Picture of Dorian Gray." 2005–11–05.
<http://imdb.com/title/tt0037988/>.

Essay: Morality and Immorality (The Picture of Dorian Gray and A Streetcar Named Desire)

by Nataniel Lessnick
March 01, 2003

The measure of a manâ ™s character is what he would do if he knew he never would be found out.

Thomas Babington

Morality is the very foundation of goodness and the pillar of righteousness. Immorality, however, is the threshold towards conspicuous malevolence. These two extremes are often but a step between which we are baffled and bemused. Morals undeniably establish the confinements of oneâ ™s behaviour in any given society. Should these principles crumble, ethical boundaries would give way to anarchical freedom. Both works explored in this analysis illustrate the succumbing to immoral conduct for selfish purposes. In The Picture of Dorian Gray, by Oscar Wilde, we are intrigued by a charming Englishman who discards his innocence and embraces loathsome hedonism. Tennessee Williamsâ ™ A Streetcar Named Desire confronts us with a stout and virile figure who abides to no opposing authority than his own. Two unscrupulous characters surface from different worlds with the equivalent dismissal of moral values common to humankind. Although one is characterised by beauty and the other, by potency, they share the same vivid animation of unrestrained cruelty. It is in their ominous acts that their factual embodiment is exposed. Wilde and Williams reveal, through these depraved beings, the basis of humanityâ ™s intrinsic flaw: the loss of inhibitions. I will further discuss, by means of relevant characters, the yearning for moral ideals as well as the clinging onto immoral philosophies.

Oscar Wildeâ ™s The Picture of Dorian Gray is set during the late nineteenth century England, a period marked with the exceeding importance of social stature and personal image. The protagonist, Dorian Gray, rises as the archetype of male pulchritude and youth. His aristocracy and stunning beauty enthral his surroundings. He often poses for Basil Hallward, an artist of great talent whose art is inspired by Dorianâ ™s charisma. While Basilâ ™s most prodigious painting is in the midst of being completed, Dorian is introduced to Lord Henry Wotton, a cynical philosopher and skilful orator. Dorian is easily seduced by his manipulative tongue and his scornful theories. Wotton envisions fashioning, corrupting the vulnerable boy into an unrelenting hedonist. Through him, Dorian faces the harsh realisation that his physical attributes are ever fading. Upon this sudden insight, he dreads the physical burden of ageing. He envies the perpetual attractiveness of Basilâ ™s masterpiece. â œ...If it were only the other way! If it were I who was to be always young, and the picture that was to grow old! For that – for that – I would give everything! Yes, there is nothing in the whole world I would not give! I would give my soul for that!â ? (Wilde p. 31). The materialisation of this wish and the metamorphosis it will ensue are to bring his demise.

Dorianâ ™s figure remains immaculate while the picture bears his abhorrent transformation. This is first confirmed following his amorous liaison with Sibyl Vane, an actress he meets at an infamous theatre. Like him, she is characterised by an entrancing beauty and a youthful naivety. Mesmerised by one another, they promptly exchange vows of fidelity. Dorian invites Henry and Basil to the theatre, if only to be dreadfully embarrassed by Sibylâ ™s artificial performance. In a fit of anger yet unknown to him, Dorian reluctantly reprimands his fiance. â œâ ¡You are shallow and stupid. My God! How mad I was to love you! What a fool I have been! You are nothing to me nowâ ¡â ? (Wilde p. 98). This vindictive refusal leads to her suicide. Upon returning to his dwelling, he is bewildered by a hideous discovery: his portrait had slightly altered, hinting the sinful transfiguration that would occur throughout his debauched existence.

Dorian conveys strong feelings of contrition upon learning of Sibylâ ™s needless death. He is conscious of his wrongdoing and feels profoundly culpable. However, Lord Henry encourages him to discard the incident and to revel in his present freedom. Dorian is torn apart as his egoism weighs heavily over his conscience. By overlooking the death he caused and indulging in pleasure, Dorian incarnates Lord Henryâ ™s philosophy. With the knowledge of his physical imperviousness to the aftermath of any consequence, he adopts hedonistic values. The complete denial of responsibility in Sibylâ ™s death is but the beginning of his moral degradation. He relishes in observing the mutilation of the picture, thus his soul. His further meetings with Henry simply magnify this descent into profligacy. â œ...You were the most unspoiled creature in the whole world. Now, I donâ ™t know what has come over you. You talk as if you had no heart, no pity in you. It is all Harryâ ™s influence. I see thatâ ¡â ? (Wilde p. 120) From then on, Dorian progressively mingles with sin; provoking scandals, visiting opium dens and frequenting prostitutes.

Dorian often gazes at the painting with horror, but is unable to divert from this lifestyle, aroused by its wickedness. He is undoubtedly aware of his ethical dissipation and, despite the beautiful items in which he surrounds himself, is appalled by the ugliness of his soul. â œ...He knew that he had tarnished himself, filled his mind with corruption, and given horror to his fancy; that he had been an evil influence to others, and had experienced a terrible joy in being soâ ¡â ? (Wilde p. 241) Dorianâ ™s fear of his predicament being discovered grows as the tableau alters with every misdeed. Although it is hidden from prying eyes, the bareness of his soul is ever–present in his mind. His hot–tempered murder of Basil not only signifies the peak of his immoral demeanour, but his obliteration of moral barriers. His iniquitous act throws him in a state of guilt–ridden paranoia. He is world–weary and borne down by the weight of this infamy.

Wildeâ ™s protagonist was not a villainous nor unprincipled man, simply pliable and somewhat narcissist. Under Lord Henryâ ™s overwhelming influence and the portraitâ ™s enticing protection, he succumbs to a world free of restrictions, tempted by self–gratification. When breaking apart from the moral confines that establish order, Dorian is thrust into a chaotic freedom. Without the ubiquitous prison that symbolises morality, anarchy and evilness reign, destroying the goodness in oneâ ™s nature. When he strikes the diabolical picture, beleaguered by remorse and maddened by regret, he wishes to purge his soul and reacquire the proper values that once governed his life. Therefore, by destroying the wantonness that marred his spirit and the guilt that plagued his conscience, he kills himself.

Lord Henry is an extremely patronizing and cynical character. His actions are not as overtly sinful as Dorianâ ™s, since he is not shielded from their repercussions. Although preaching hedonism, he never acts on his philosophies, remaining within the boundaries of what society deems tolerable. He thus has little knowledge of the pragmatic effects induced by his philosophy. He is portrayed as a coward, utilising Dorian to make flesh of his theories, but not venturing on them himself for fear of ruining his social figure. He is a brilliant intellect, although he has a narrow understanding of human behaviour. For instance, when he asserts : â œâ ¦All crime is vulgar, just as all vulgarity is crime. It is not in you, Dorian to commit a murder...â ? (Wilde p. 234), he is entirely oblivious to Dorianâ ™s tragedy.

While most of humanity is constrained to moral hindrances, there are those who drift away from these ideals, and become the source of misdemeanours2E Although morality and ethics are restraining concepts, they shelter the individual and thus, mankind. Without them, there could only be degradation and self–destruction, as illustrated by Oscar Wilde in The Picture of Dorian Gray. As Mahatma Gandhi once said : â œThe human voice can never reach the distance that is covered by the still small voice of conscience.â ? One may enjoy life and have no fear from death if he obeys his scruples.

Tennessee Williamsâ ™ A Streetcar Named Desire formulates a medium to reflect upon the morbid aspects of humanity and the result of these societal downfalls. Stanley Kowalski emerges from an impoverished rural setting in New Orleans as the epitome of flagrant barbarity. His speech is coarsely uneducated and his actions display instinctive crudeness. He adheres to mankindâ ™s most primitive rule and basic code: to hunt or be hunted. His household symbolizes his territory and anyone who menaces this tenure should be eliminated. The metaphorical episode in which he casually tosses to Stella, his wife, a bundle of bloody meat emphasises his ape–like qualities. He has little notion of courteousness, which understandably repulse his pampered sister–in–law, Blanche.

The image of a delicate flower amongst a mound of litter is comparable to Blanche Duboisâ ™ arrival at the Kowalski household. â œâ ¦Her expression is of shocked disbelief. Her appearance is incongruous to this settingâ ¦â ? (Williams p. 15). She appears inherently refined and somewhat ostentatious, having seemingly never witnessed indignity. However, her false decorum is a rather deliberate effort to save herself from misery. Blanche exists in a self–fabricated universe in which she blinds herself from realityâ ™s bleakness. Her haughty manners contrast with Stanleyâ ™s uncouth behaviour and clash from their first encounter.

Stanley imposes his animalistic vigour upon Blanche since he feels threatened by her presence. He despises her aristocratic ways, her diminutive expressions concerning his origin and her dallying about with his friend Mitch. His hatred of Blanche is intensified by her unflattering dialogue with Stella. â œHe acts like an animal, has an animalâ ™s habits! Eats like one, moves like one, talks like one! Thereâ ™s even something – sub–human – something not quite to the stage of humanity yet!â !â ? (Williams p. 72). This culmination of anger is manifested in his enquiry of her promiscuous past and in his spiteful birthday gift. He relentlessly thwarts her relationship with Mitch, sabotaging her illusions of rescue. In his vile quest to bring Blancheâ ™s ruin, he brutally exposes her to the harshness of her position.

Stanleyâ ™s final effort in tarnishing Blancheâ ™s image is animated by chauvinism. Although his past attempts were strictly psychological blows, he now wishes to exert physical power upon her. In Blancheâ ™s state of vulnerability, he rapes her, devastating the remainder of her sanity. His degenerate character, first insinuated after hitting his pregnant wife, is given full evidence following this acrimonious sin. The concluding scene consists of Blanche being ostracised to an asylum and the depiction of Stanley as the dedicated husband, soothing his wife as she embraces their newborn child. The fallaciousness of this image, given what we have learned throughout the play, paradoxically brings into perspective societyâ ™s erroneous conception of right and wrong.

The settings of The Picture of Dorian Gray and of A Streetcar Named Desire differ immensely. Dorian is immersed in a tumultuous social environment, caught in the intricate web of social demeanour. Stanley, on the other hand, resides in a modest yet impecunious milieu. In Wildeâ ™s work, the innocent is poisoned, succumbing to immoral growth and subsiding into internal deterioration. In Williamsâ ™ play, remorseless animosity is the dominating asset, as modern manâ ™s conduct is banished. Although these events take place at nearly a centuryâ ™s interval, one remaining constant is observed : the consequences on the self and on others resulting from the dismissal of morals.

Dorian and Stanley are above all human, and as every human, are subjected to the similar dilemma: to remain within the borders of moral beliefs, or to venture across into immoral conditions. The laws of ethics impose restrictions and greatly limit humankindâ ™s actions, but allow the worldâ ™s proper functioning. Both characters break free from this psychological incarceration and therefore, represent the dark side of human nature.

It is critical that we, as a community, comprehend the necessity to abide by the restraining order of morals. Only then will violence and havoc cease to exist. Is it not in our power to differentiate the good from the bad? This question lies not underneath a compulsory set of rules, but rather within the depths of our conscience. Wilde and Williams have magnified, through their enlightening characters, the step between morality and immorality. In the end, it is in our hands to decide on which to stand.

Essay: The Life of Secrecy

by Anonymous
October 01, 2003

In The Picture of Dorian Gray, Oscar Wilde writes of a beautiful young man with an ugly secret. While Dorian Gray will forever retain the innocent looks of his youth, his portrait will degenerate with every wrong he commits. Unburdened and unmarked by his corruption, Dorian behaves as he wills, performing numerous unspeakable acts that he must never expose. Throughout the novel, Wilde explores the theme of the power of secrecy, of which Dorian is only one example. In addition to driving Dorian to hideous crimes, secrecy also wields enormous influence over all the major characters. It dictates their relations to each other, is the impetus behind their actions, and even determines their death hour.

Secrecy is the foundation of all romantic relationships in the novel. "When one is in love, one always begins by deceiving oneself, and one always ends by deceiving others" (Wilde, 197). Of marriage, Lord Henry states: "the one charm of marriage is that it makes a life of deception absolutely necessary for both parties" (Wilde, 143). Though Lord Henry's assertions are always doubtful, it does appear that his wife Victoria knows very little about him. "I always hear Harry's view from his friends. It is the only way I get to know of them" (Wilde, 190). Dorian's relationship with Sybil Vane is certainly no exception. Dorian falls in love not with her, but with the characters she transforms into on stage. "Never... is she Sibyl Vane" (Wilde, 200). However, when she reveals her true self to Dorian and acts badly, Dorian is furious with disappointment. "You have killed my love... You have spoiled the romance of my life" (Wilde, 237). It seems that before Sybil reveals her true nature, Dorian can fancy her as he wishes, and believe her to be any tragic heroine of Shakespeare's devising. However, when she shows herself to be nothing but a naive child, she kills all his possibilities of fantasy. "You used to stir my imagination. Now you don't even stir my curiosity" (Wilde, 236). Dorian dissolves the relationship when there is no longer the fantasy and mystery created by the secrecy of Sybil's true nature.

In addition to romantic relations, secrecy serves as a binding force for all the characters in the novel. Initially, Dorian is accepted among high society because no one knows of his true nature. They believe in his innocent face and think him charming beyond measure, completely oblivious to his secret corruption. However, as rumors circulate of his immoral ways, "these whispered scandals only increased in the eyes of many, his strange and dangerous charm" (Wilde, 299). They are aware that he leads a secret life of crime, but know little of the details. Thus they are even more interested in him because his secrecy gives him a certain allure, a certain aura of mystery.

However, the discovery of these secrets marks the end of these relations. For those who only hear rumors of Dorian's crimes, his secrecy adds a certain charm to his character. However, those who have full knowledge of his corruptions, "those who had been most intimate with him appeared... to shun him" (Wilde, 299). When one of Dorian's secrets is unveiled, they are forced to face the reality of his character, which is anything but charming. They are no longer drawn to him because they have seen his soul in its nude, wicked form, which leaves no possibility for anything pleasant. Dorian is well aware of the necessity of hiding the details of his secrets, becoming ever so paranoid lest anyone should discover the painting, fearing that once the secret is revealed, he would lose all his friends and relations. "You (Lord Henry) don't know everything about me. I think that if you did, even you would turn from me" (Wilde, 394).

The clearest demonstration of both the attraction and finality of secrecy can be seen in Alan Campbell. As Dorian begins to tell him about Basil's murder, Alan refuses to hear anymore. "Stop, Gray. I don't want to know anything further... I entirely decline to be mixed up in your life" (Wilde, 328). This suggests that Alan realizes that knowledge of his secrets would surely draw him to Dorian and intertwine their lives again, just as others are drawn to his mysteriousness. However, he is blackmailed by Dorian into helping him rid the evidence of the murder. The narrative does not give details of this exchange, but it can be assumed that the letter Dorian writes and threatens to send would reveal some secret of Alan's. However, after he performs the monstrous deed, he shoots himself one night in his laboratory, unable to bear the burden of what has now become both his and Dorian's secret. Thus, indirectly, his knowledge of Dorian's secrets, and Dorian's knowledge of his, not only ends their current relationship but also eliminates any possibility for such in the future.

All the major characters of the novel are described in relation to their secrets. For example, Basil is introduced as an artist strangely and secretly drawn to Dorian. Lord Henry is defined by his secret motive to experiment with Dorian. It can therefore be said that these secrets not only characterize, but also take control over the actions of these characters in the novel. Thus it would seem natural that secrecy holds the key to the life of its bearer. The unveiling of one's secret represents his death. When Dorian threatens to reveal Alan Campbell's secret, Alan "felt as if his heart was beating itself to death in some empty hollow" (Wilde, 332). He has little choice but to comply with Dorian's demands because of the threat that is posed to his life. The importance of secrecy now becomes a major factor in his decisions and actions. Similarly, when Basil suggests various ways to absolve Dorian of the corruption that the painting depicts – an attempt to erase Dorian's secret, Dorian suddenly erupts with "the mad passions of a hunted animal" (Wilde, 319). The comparison to the hunted animal suggests that Basil is a great menace to Dorian's life. His desire to rid him of his secrets poses a threat to his very existence. Faced with Basil's threat to his secret and his life, Dorian has no choice but to murder him, again carrying out what secrecy demands of him.

Perhaps the best example of the symbol of death as an unveiling of secrecy lies in Dorian's own death. Hoping to "kill the past" and erase all his secret sins, he stabs the picture (Wilde, 390). However, rather than killing the picture and freeing himself from all the secrets it holds, he instead kills himself, and becomes marked by his own corruption while the picture is absolved. This transformation can be seen as an unveiling of his secret. The depravity of his soul, which has been concealed by the painting for so long, finally shows through his corpse. Dorian Gray's death coincides with the exposure of his secret criminality.

However, even this unveiling of Dorian's biggest secret can be seen as another way in which the secret is propagating. From beginning to end, the text is a revelation of a series of secrets, but each revelation is replaced by another secret. Dorian's whole life is an effort to conceal something, but that something is constantly changing. First he covers his involvement in Sybil Vane's death. Upon discovering the secret of the portrait, he locks it inside the attic. He lies about his bad reputation to Basil, only later to reveal to him his soul. He murders him and tries to erase all evidence of it. The list goes on and on. Even in death, his secrecy continues. Though the corruption of Dorian's soul will be visible for the world to see, the secret of the portrait, as well as the details of his death, will forever remain a mystery to others. The transformation of the corpse and the portrait creates even more mystery surrounding Dorian Gray. In the end, when Dorian decides to do away with the portrait that holds all his secrets, the secrets seems to wield power over him, and reject the end chosen by their bearer. Even in his death, his secrets seem to propagate.

Though Lord Henry is in no way an admirable character, it must be said that he is a very smart one. He is the only character in the novel who understands the workings of secrets. Initially, he manipulates Dorian into opening up to him completely. "You could not have helped telling me, Dorian. All through your life you will tell me everything you do" (Wilde, 197). However, after having achieved this goal, he backs away, and soon becomes oblivious to Dorian's affairs. When Dorian tells him that he's murdered Basil, he replies: "you were posing for a character that doesn't suit you... It is not in you, Dorian, to commit a murder" (Wilde, 379). Lord Henry seems to care little about the details of one's secrets, but only chooses to probe enough to make life a little more interesting. Unlike Sybil, who reveals too much of her secret too soon, unlike Basil, who digs too deeply, and unlike Alan and Dorian, who refuse to acknowledge secrecy's perpetual existence, Lord Henry lets secrecy take its own course. Thus he is the only major character in the novel who escapes tragedy.

In The Picture of Dorian Gray, secrecy represents a driving force behind many aspects of the novel. Secrecy seems to have a life of its own, and control the relations, actions, as well as the existence, of its bearers. In the opening pages of the novel, Wilde writes that "secrecy seems to be the one thing that can make modern life mysterious or marvelous to us. The commonest thing is delightful if one only hides it" (Wilde, 143). This certainly seems to hold true throughout the novel. It is secrecy that draws so many to Dorian Gray and heightens his charms. However, as secrets are revealed, people pull away from him because he no longer generates interest or mystery. In addition to being a source of seduction for the characters in the novel, it also functions in the same way towards the readers. Thus secrecy must always regenerate itself, even at the cost of fatality to the characters to maintain readers' interest.

Quiz 1

1. **To which play does Dorian take Henry and Basil?**
   A. A Midsummer Night's Dream
   B. Dr. Faustus
   C. The Importance of Being Earnest
   D. Romeo &Juliet

2. **Who is the only person that Dorian shows the painting to?**
   A. Basil Hallward
   B. Sybil Vane
   C. Lord Henry Wotton
   D. Alan Campbell

3. **About how many years elapse between the death of Sybil Vane and the death of her brother?**
   A. 3
   B. 13
   C. 18
   D. 38

4. **Who does Dorian meet in the opium den?**
   A. Ernest Bunberry
   B. Lord Henry
   C. Adrian Singleton
   D. Alan Campbell

5. **Which composer wrote the nocturne that Dorian plays for Lord Henry?**
   A. Chopin
   B. Dorian's father
   C. Schubert
   D. Beethoven

6. **What gift from Lord Henry does Dorian blame for playing a large part in his corruption?**
   A. a novel
   B. a book of poetry
   C. a handheld mirror
   D. a box of opium

7. **What instrument does Dorian play?**
    A. violin
    B. clarinet
    C. oboe
    D. piano

8. **What is James Vane's occupation?**
    A. sailor
    B. soldier
    C. spy
    D. actor

9. **In the preface, Wilde states that "It is [. . .], and not life that art really mirrors." Fill in the blank.**
    A. "Caliban"
    B. "the spectator"
    C. "society"
    D. "the artist"

10. **How does Basil Hallward die?**
    A. he is run over by his train to Paris
    B. he is stabbed by Dorian
    C. he is shot in a hunting accident
    D. he poisons himself

11. **Why does Dorian stop loving Sybil?**
    A. she gives a bad performance
    B. she sees the portrait
    C. she is disfigured
    D. she has a murderously jealous brother

12. **Where does Basil publicly display the titular painting of Dorian?**
    A. nowhere
    B. The Royal Academy
    C. Grosvenor
    D. The Conservatory

13. **What does Basil confess to Dorian?**
    A. that he knows the truth about the painting
    B. that he wants to sleep with him
    C. that he adores him
    D. that he loves Henry

14. **How does Dorian hide the painting?**
    A. he places it behind a mirror
    B. he arranges to have it stolen
    C. he locks it in the attic
    D. he locks it in the basement

15. **What does Lord Henry claim to value more than anything else?**
    A. beauty
    B. love
    C. money
    D. truth

16. **Why doesn't Basil want to exhibit the painting?**
    A. he feels that he's put too much of himself into it
    B. he doesn't want other people to see Dorian
    C. he considers it to be an artistic failure
    D. he has enchanted it

17. **What is Mrs. Vane's profession?**
    A. singer
    B. actress
    C. chef
    D. prostitute

18. **Where does Dorian first see Sybil?**
    A. on the street
    B. in the theater
    C. in an opium den
    D. at a party

19. **What is the name of Dorian's grandfather?**
    A. Lord Gray
    B. Lord Kelso
    C. Lord Fermor
    D. Lord Wotton

20. **How old is Dorian when Basil completes the painting?**
    A. 18
    B. 20
    C. 23
    D. 25

21. **Where was Basil headed on the night of his death?**
    A. Vienna
    B. Prague
    C. Amsterdam
    D. Paris

22. **What is the name of Dorian's servant, whom he dismisses?**
    A. Jeeves
    B. Victor
    C. Alfonse
    D. Oscar

23. **Finish the phrase from the preface: "All art is quite [...]"**
    A. useful
    B. useless
    C. admirable
    D. beautiful

24. **How long does Dorian mourn for Sybil before going out with Lord Henry?**
    A. several hours
    B. one year
    C. eighteen years
    D. three weeks

25. Who kills Dorian?
   A. Dorian
   B. James Vane
   C. he never dies
   D. Alan Campbell

Quiz 1 Answer Key

1. **(D)** Romeo &Juliet
2. **(A)** Basil Hallward
3. **(C)** 18
4. **(C)** Adrian Singleton
5. **(A)** Chopin
6. **(A)** a novel
7. **(D)** piano
8. **(A)** sailor
9. **(B)** "the spectator"
10. **(B)** he is stabbed by Dorian
11. **(A)** she gives a bad performance
12. **(A)** nowhere
13. **(C)** that he adores him
14. **(C)** he locks it in the attic
15. **(A)** beauty
16. **(A)** he feels that he's put too much of himself into it
17. **(B)** actress
18. **(B)** in the theater
19. **(B)** Lord Kelso
20. **(B)** 20
21. **(D)** Paris
22. **(B)** Victor
23. **(B)** useless
24. **(A)** several hours
25. **(A)** Dorian

Quiz 2

1. **What causes the picture's appearance to change, instead of Dorian's?**
    A. a pact with Mephistopheles
    B. a botched science experiment
    C. Dorian's wish
    D. Basil's enchantment

2. **What does Dorian do right after abandoning Sybil at the theater?**
    A. he goes to the opera with Lord Henry
    B. he goes to an opium den
    C. he confesses his love to Hetty Merton
    D. he wanders the streets until dawn and returns home

3. **With what name did Wilde sign the preface?**
    A. Anonymous
    B. Oscar Wilde
    C. Dorian Gray
    D. Henry Wotton

4. **What, according to Lord Henry, is the secret to always looking young?**
    A. sow corruption among the youths you encounter
    B. bathe in warm milk twice a week
    C. never listen to bad music
    D. never have an unbecoming emotion

5. **How does Mrs. Wotton, according to what she tells Dorian, familiarize herself with her husband's views?**
    A. she never talks when he is talking
    B. she reads his weekly articles in the paper
    C. she hears his friends state them
    D. she reads his diary

6. **What, according to Dorian, is one obligated to do when bad music is being played?**
    A. throw rotten vegetables
    B. leave immediately
    C. freely converse with those around you
    D. patiently sit through it

7. What gets shot by sir Geoffrey at the conservatory?
A. a rabbit and a man
B. a deer and a raven
C. a pheasant and a dog
D. a window and the picture of Dorian

8. How does Sybil die?
A. she swallows poison
B. Dorian strangles her
C. she jumps off a bridge
D. she stabs herself

9. What subject does Dorian NOT immerse himself in?
A. jewelry
B. medicine
C. mysticism
D. music

10. Why is Basil determined to see Dorian on the night of his death?
A. to confront him about the awful rumors he's heard
B. to acquire opium
C. to warn him about the painting's enchantment
D. to get him to pose for a portrait one last time

11. How does James Vane recognize Dorian?
A. from the nickname "Prince Charming"
B. he recognizes his face from the painting
C. he had heard his voice once, when eavesdropping on Sybil
D. he had seen him riding in a carriage years before

12. What color is Dorian's hair?
A. red
B. black
C. blond
D. brown

13. **Who introduces Dorian and Henry?**
    A. Lord Kelso
    B. Lady Agatha
    C. Basil
    D. Sybil

14. **Why does Dorian call on Alan Campbell?**
    A. to apologize for hurting him
    B. to invite him to dinner
    C. to blackmail his father
    D. to dispose of a dead body

15. **How old is Dorian when Basil dies?**
    A. thirty–eight
    B. thirty–three
    C. twenty
    D. forty–two

16. **What first changes about the portrait?**
    A. the hands grow red with blood
    B. a smirk appears
    C. the eyes wrinkle
    D. the hair lengthens

17. **Finish the statement form the preface: "To reveal [...] and conceal the artist is art's aim."**
    A. beauty
    B. art
    C. life
    D. truth

18. **How do Dorian's servants enter the attic after hearing the scream?**
    A. by using the secret entrance in the study
    B. by kicking down the door
    C. by climbing through the window
    D. by unlocking the door with a secret key

19. **What does Sybil promise Dorian not to tell people about him?**
    A. his intentions to marry her
    B. his social class
    C. his real name
    D. that his portrait is aging

20. **What gift from Henry does Dorian destroy in the final chapter?**
    A. a porcelain sculpture
    B. a old novel
    C. a hand–held mirror
    D. the painting

21. **Who hosts the party at the conservatory at Selby Royal?**
    A. Dorian
    B. The Duchess of Monmouth
    C. Lord Henry
    D. Lady Agatha

22. **What does Dorian see through the window that makes him faint?**
    A. A dagger floating in thin air
    B. The face of Basil Hallward
    C. His own face, only old and wrinkled
    D. The face of James Vane

23. **On which night does Dorian encounter Basil for the last time?**
    A. Christmas Eve
    B. March 15th
    C. October 31st
    D. November 9th

24. **How does Dorian dispose of Basil's belongings?**
    A. he trades them for opium
    B. he hides them in the attic
    C. he sinks them in the river
    D. he burns them

25. **What is Henry Wotton's title?**
    A. Sir
    B. Duke
    C. Lord
    D. Count

Quiz 2 Answer Key

1. **(C)** Dorian's wish
2. **(D)** he wanders the streets until dawn and returns home
3. **(B)** Oscar Wilde
4. **(D)** never have an unbecoming emotion
5. **(C)** she hears his friends state them
6. **(C)** freely converse with those around you
7. **(A)** a rabbit and a man
8. **(A)** she swallows poison
9. **(B)** medicine
10. **(A)** to confront him about the awful rumors he's heard
11. **(A)** from the nickname "Prince Charming"
12. **(C)** blond
13. **(C)** Basil
14. **(D)** to dispose of a dead body
15. **(A)** thirty–eight
16. **(B)** a smirk appears
17. **(B)** art
18. **(C)** by climbing through the window
19. **(C)** his real name
20. **(C)** a hand–held mirror
21. **(A)** Dorian
22. **(D)** The face of James Vane
23. **(D)** November 9th
24. **(D)** he burns them
25. **(C)** Lord

Quiz 3

1. **With what sort of instrumentalist did Henry's wife run away?**
   A. a cellist
   B. a pianist
   C. a flutist
   D. a violinist

2. **How does Alan Campbell die?**
   A. he is murdered by Dorian
   B. he is accidentally shot
   C. he is killed by a trolley
   D. he commits suicide

3. **Which of the following words best describes James Vane?**
   A. stocky
   B. forgiving
   C. lean
   D. tall

4. **What had Dorian just finished doing when he hears the news of Sybil's death?**
   A. writing a letter to her father, asking for her hand
   B. writing an apologetic letter to her
   C. writing a sonnet to her
   D. writing an angry letter to her

5. **Where does Lord Henry first instill corruption in Dorian?**
   A. at the theater
   B. at a party of his aunt's
   C. in Basil's garden
   D. in Dorian's chamber

6. **Why does Basil want to speak with Dorian before leaving the country?**
   A. to confront him about rumors
   B. to damn him
   C. to kill him
   D. to confess his love

7. **Who does Dorian accompany hunting?**
   A. Sir William
   B. Sir Carlton
   C. Sir Mixalot
   D. Sir Geoffrey

8. **Why is Mrs Vane disappointed by her son's exit?**
   A. he fails to hug his sister good–bye
   B. it isn't sufficiently dramatic
   C. he leaves in the company of another man
   D. he doesn't kiss her good–bye

9. **What color is the binding of the novel that Lord Henry gives to Dorian, and which the youth becomes obsessed with?**
   A. yellow
   B. red
   C. blue
   D. black

10. **Where does Lord Henry want Dorian to go, instead of staying at home and mourning for Sybil?**
    A. to an opium den
    B. to a play
    C. to a garden
    D. to the opera

11. **Fill in the blank in this quote: "there is nothing that [. . .] cannot express."**
    A. Actors
    B. Artists
    C. Man
    D. Art

12. **Why do Dorian's friends largely ignore the rumors about him?**
    A. because Basil tells them that the rumors are false
    B. because the rumors are untrue
    C. because Dorian is so beautiful
    D. because Lord Henry pays them off

13. **Which character did not appear in the original edition of the novel?**
    A. Victor
    B. James Vane
    C. Lord Henry
    D. Basil

14. **How many children does Mrs Vane have when we first meet her?**
    A. one
    B. two
    C. three
    D. seven

15. **What is Lord Henry's relation to Basil Hallward?**
    A. step brother
    B. friend
    C. cousin
    D. half brother

16. **How do Dorian's servants recognize his body?**
    A. by his clothes
    B. by his beautiful hair
    C. by his necklaces
    D. by the rings on his fingers

17. **Which of these characters never touches a knife?**
    A. Dorian
    B. Basil
    C. James
    D. Sybil

18. **How does Mrs Wotton say she learns of her husband's views?**
    A. through his friends
    B. talking in bed
    C. through the letters he writes to her
    D. she reads them in the paper

19. **Finish the quote: "The secret of remaining young is [...]"**
    A. never to have an emotion that is unbecoming
    B. never to read an American novel
    C. never to dine alone
    D. always to indulge your passions

20. **What does Sybil call Dorian?**
    A. Prince Charming
    B. Sir Gawain
    C. Immortal Beloved
    D. Sugarplumb

21. **What nickname does Dorian give to Lord Henry at a party?**
    A. Harmful Henry
    B. Wotton the Wit
    C. Prince Paradox
    D. King Corruption

22. **What character never seems to receive any comeuppance for his behavior?**
    A. Dorian
    B. Lord Henry
    C. Basil
    D. James

23. **What word best describes Sybil?**
    A. cunning
    B. innocent
    C. dishonest
    D. headstrong

24. **What word does NOT desribe Lord Henry?**
    A. clever
    B. manipulative
    C. compassionate
    D. smug

25. What social quirk is Basil noted for?
A. smoking colored cigarettes

B. being always drunk in public

C. wearing a beret

D. not appearing in public for months at a time

Quiz 3 Answer Key

1. **(B)** a pianist
2. **(D)** he commits suicide
3. **(A)** stocky
4. **(B)** writing an apologetic letter to her
5. **(C)** in Basil's garden
6. **(A)** to confront him about rumors
7. **(D)** Sir Geoffrey
8. **(B)** it isn't sufficiently dramatic
9. **(A)** yellow
10. **(D)** to the opera
11. **(D)** Art
12. **(C)** because Dorian is so beautiful
13. **(B)** James Vane
14. **(B)** two
15. **(B)** friend
16. **(D)** by the rings on his fingers
17. **(D)** Sybil
18. **(A)** through his friends
19. **(A)** never to have an emotion that is unbecoming
20. **(A)** Prince Charming
21. **(C)** Prince Paradox
22. **(B)** Lord Henry
23. **(B)** innocent
24. **(C)** compassionate
25. **(D)** not appearing in public for months at a time

Quiz 4

1. **Which of these characters has the least amount of disposable income?**
    A. Dorian
    B. James Vane
    C. Adrian Singleton
    D. Basil

2. **Who tells James the truth about Dorian's age?**
    A. an old blind man drinking in the opium den
    B. two women standing outside of the opium den
    C. Sir Geoffrey, outside of the pub
    D. Lord Hallward, at the party

3. **By the end of the novel, which of these would Dorian never have collected?**
    A. exotic drapes and murals
    B. exotic gems
    C. exotic birds
    D. exotic books

4. **Who states that "the only things one never regrets are one's mistakes?"**
    A. Dorian
    B. Lord Henry
    C. Alan
    D. Basil

5. **What person did Henry see in the park, as he informs Dorian in chapter 19?**
    A. a lunatic
    B. a preacher
    C. Basil
    D. an older version of Dorian

6. **What type of composition does Dorian play for Lord Henry in chapter 19?**
    A. sonata
    B. concerto
    C. nocturne
    D. overture

7. **Why does Dorian expect the picture to have changed for the better in the final chapter?**
   A. he stopped himself from corrupting a young girl
   B. he went to confession
   C. he vowed never to see Lord Henry again
   D. he gave lots of money to a beggar

8. **What sort of an expression does Dorian find in the portrait before trying to destroy it?**
   A. a hypocritical smirk
   B. a languid stare
   C. an apathetic pout
   D. a damnable grimace

9. **What sort of death never occurs in the novel?**
   A. hanging
   B. stabbing
   C. drowning
   D. poisoning

10. **What is the name of the girl whom Dorian refrains from corrupting?**
    A. Ingrid Cambell
    B. Harriet Wotton
    C. Matty Harton
    D. Hetty Merton

11. **What phrase best describes Basil?**
    A. conniving
    B. sensitive
    C. rude
    D. boisterous

12. **Why did Oscar Wilde rewrite parts of the novel?**
    A. to enhance Dorian's character
    B. to remove the homosexual undertones
    C. to transform it into a love letter to his wife
    D. because he thought it was sub–par

13. **Who raised Dorian?**
    A. his grandfather
    B. his grandmother
    C. his father
    D. his mother

14. **From who did Dorian inherit his money?**
    A. a widowed aunt
    B. his grandfather
    C. Lord Henry
    D. his father

15. **Who hosts the event at which James Vane is killed?**
    A. Dorian
    B. The Duchess of Monmouth
    C. Lord Henry
    D. Lord Fermor

16. **What type of wildlife does Sir Geoffrey shoot?**
    A. a rabbit
    B. a squirrel
    C. a deer
    D. a chimpanzee

17. **How does the narrator refer to the body of Basil Hallward?**
    A. "hideous corpse"
    B. "twisted carcass"
    C. "hateful portrait"
    D. "thing"

18. **How does Dorian convince Alan Campbell to help him?**
    A. lots of money
    B. an invitation to an exclusive party
    C. blackmail
    D. a promise of opium

19. On what terms do Dorian and Alan Campbell part ways?
A. Dorian throws Alan out of his house
B. Alan vows to kill Dorian
C. Alan never wants to see him again
D. They make amends and plan to attend the opera together

20. Whose life doesn't Dorian ruin?
A. Alan Singleton
B. Sybil Vane
C. Adrian Singleton
D. Alan Campbell

21. What word does NOT describe the Duchess of Monmouth
A. flirtatious
B. chaste
C. clever
D. charming

22. Under what conditions would Dorian pose for another of Basil's portraits?
A. under no conditions
B. if Basil undoes the enchantment of the portrait
C. if Basil agrees never to display any portraits of Dorian
D. if Basil promises never to speak of his love for Dorian again

23. What did Wilde refer to as the "note of doom" that runs through the novel "like purple thread"?
A. references to opium
B. thinly veiled parodies of public figures
C. arguments supporting "intelligent design"
D. homosexual undertones

24. In what periodical did the first version of the novel appear?
A. Lippincott's Monthly
B. Rolling Stone Mason's Monthly
C. The Westminster Review
D. The Royal Gentleman's Quarterly

25. **What is one of the events that prompts people to forget about Basil Hallward's disappearance?**
    A. Dorian's mysterious behavior
    B. Sybil Vane's death
    C. the question of who shot Mr. Burns
    D. Lord Henry's divorce

Quiz 4 Answer Key

1. **(B)** James Vane
2. **(B)** two women standing outside of the opium den
3. **(C)** exotic birds
4. **(B)** Lord Henry
5. **(B)** a preacher
6. **(C)** nocturne
7. **(A)** he stopped himself from corrupting a young girl
8. **(A)** a hypocritical smirk
9. **(C)** drowning
10. **(D)** Hetty Merton
11. **(B)** sensitive
12. **(B)** to remove the homosexual undertones
13. **(A)** his grandfather
14. **(B)** his grandfather
15. **(A)** Dorian
16. **(A)** a rabbit
17. **(D)** "thing"
18. **(C)** blackmail
19. **(C)** Alan never wants to see him again
20. **(A)** Alan Singleton
21. **(B)** chaste
22. **(A)** under no conditions
23. **(D)** homosexual undertones
24. **(A)** Lippincott's Monthly
25. **(D)** Lord Henry's divorce

ClassicNotes

Getting you the grade since 1999™

Other ClassicNotes from GradeSaver™

1984
Absalom, Absalom
Adam Bede
The Adventures of Augie
    March
The Adventures of
    Huckleberry Finn
The Adventures of Tom
    Sawyer
The Aeneid
Agamemnon
The Age of Innocence
Alice in Wonderland
All My Sons
All Quiet on the Western
    Front
All the King's Men
All the Pretty Horses
The Ambassadors
American Beauty
Angela's Ashes
Animal Farm
Anna Karenina
Antigone
Antony and Cleopatra
Aristotle's Ethics
Aristotle's Poetics
Aristotle's Politics
As I Lay Dying
As You Like It
The Awakening
Babbitt
The Bacchae
Bartleby the Scrivener
The Bean Trees
The Bell Jar

Beloved
Benito Cereno
Beowulf
Billy Budd
Black Boy
Bleak House
Bluest Eye
Brave New World
Breakfast at Tiffany's
Call of the Wild
Candide
The Canterbury Tales
Cat's Cradle
Catch-22
The Catcher in the Rye
The Caucasian Chalk
    Circle
The Cherry Orchard
The Chosen
A Christmas Carol
Chronicle of a Death
    Foretold
Civil Disobedience
Civilization and Its
    Discontents
A Clockwork Orange
The Color of Water
The Color Purple
Comedy of Errors
Communist Manifesto
A Confederacy of
    Dunces
Connecticut Yankee in
    King Arthur's Court
Coriolanus

The Count of Monte
    Cristo
Crime and Punishment
The Crucible
Cry, the Beloved
    Country
The Crying of Lot 49
Cymbeline
Daisy Miller
Death in Venice
Death of a Salesman
The Death of Ivan Ilych
Democracy in America
Devil in a Blue Dress
The Diary of Anne Frank
Disgrace
Divine Comedy-I:
    Inferno
A Doll's House
Don Quixote Book I
Don Quixote Book II
Dr. Faustus
Dr. Jekyll and Mr. Hyde
Dracula
Dubliners
East of Eden
Emma
Ender's Game
Endgame
Ethan Frome
The Eumenides
Everything is Illuminated
Fahrenheit 451
The Fall of the House of
    Usher
Farewell to Arms

For our full list of over 250 Study Guides, Quizzes,
Sample College Application Essays, Literature Essays and E-texts, visit:

www.gradesaver.com

ClassicNotes

GradeSaver™

Getting you the grade since 1999™

Other ClassicNotes from GradeSaver™

Othello
Our Town
Pale Fire
Paradise Lost
A Passage to India
The Pearl
The Picture of Dorian
    Gray
Poems of W.B. Yeats:
    The Rose
Portrait of the Artist as a
    Young Man
Pride and Prejudice
Prometheus Bound
Pudd'nhead Wilson
Pygmalion
Rabbit, Run
A Raisin in the Sun
The Real Life of
    Sebastian Knight
Red Badge of Courage
The Republic
Richard II
Richard III
The Rime of the Ancient
    Mariner
Robinson Crusoe
Roll of Thunder, Hear
    My Cry
Romeo and Juliet
A Room of One's Own
A Room With a View
Rosencrantz and
    Guildenstern Are
    Dead
Salome

The Scarlet Letter
Secret Sharer
Sense and Sensibility
A Separate Peace
Shakespeare's Sonnets
Siddhartha
Silas Marner
Sir Gawain and the
    Green Knight
Sister Carrie
Six Characters in Search
    of an Author
Slaughterhouse Five
Snow Falling on Cedars
The Social Contract
Something Wicked This
    Way Comes
Song of Roland
Sons and Lovers
The Sorrows of Young
    Werther
The Sound and the Fury
Spring Awakening
The Stranger
A Streetcar Named
    Desire
The Sun Also Rises
Tale of Two Cities
The Taming of the Shrew
The Tempest
Tender is the Night
Tess of the D'Urbervilles
Their Eyes Were
    Watching God
Things Fall Apart
The Threepenny Opera

The Time Machine
Titus Andronicus
To Build a Fire
To Kill a Mockingbird
To the Lighthouse
Treasure Island
Troilus and Cressida
Turn of the Screw
Twelfth Night
Ulysses
Uncle Tom's Cabin
Utopia
A Very Old Man With
    Enormous Wings
The Visit
Volpone
Waiting for Godot
Waiting for Lefty
Walden
Washington Square
Where the Red Fern
    Grows
White Fang
White Noise
White Teeth
Who's Afraid of Virginia
    Woolf
Winesburg, Ohio
The Winter's Tale
Woyzeck
Wuthering Heights
The Yellow Wallpaper
Yonnondio: From the
    Thirties

For our full list of over 250 Study Guides, Quizzes,
Sample College Application Essays, Literature Essays and E-texts, visit:

www.gradesaver.com

Made in the USA